KU-054-585

First published in Great Britain in 2003 by
YOUNG WRITERS
Remus House,
Coltsfoot Drive,
Peterborough, PE2 9JX
Telephone (01733) 890066

HB ISBN 0 75434 114 3
SB ISBN 0 75434 115 1

FOREWORD

This year, the Young Writers' Hidden Treasures competition proudly presents a showcase of the best poetic talent from over 72,000 up-and-coming writers nationwide.

Young Writers was established in 1991 and we are still successful, even in today's technologically-led world, in promoting and encouraging the reading and writing of poetry.

The thought, effort, imagination and hard work put into each poem impressed us all, and once again, the task of selecting poems was a difficult one, but nevertheless, an enjoyable experience.

We hope you are as pleased as we are with the final selection and that you and your family continue to be entertained with *Hidden Treasures Rotherham* for many years to come.

CONTENTS

Dearne Carrfield Primary School

Cody Mellor	50
James Dunn	51
Laura Green	51
Liam Highfield	52
Dominic Williamson	52
Emma Cowley	53
Rebecca Taylor	53
Emily Tarff	54
Patrick Desbrough & Brandon Crook	55
Lauren Marsh	56
Hannah King	57
Katrina Pugh	58

Dearne Goldthorpe Primary School

Brittany Beighton	58
Katie Fletcher	58
Georgina Bentham	59
Lewis Freeman	59
Jessica Bywater	60
Sadie O'Connor	60
Christopher Timmins	61
Thomas Jane	61
Alison Fletcher	62
Kirsty Suchacki	62
Bradley Whiteman	63
James Stevenson	63
Becky Jane	64
Bradley Grant	64
Chanelle Henshaw	65
Natalie Beighton	65
Sarah Jones	66
Callum Cooper	66
Zoe Iles	67
Amy Kilner	67
Gwen Tsang	68
Emma Chambers	68
Matthew Suggett	69
James Brice	69

James Jones   69

Lilly Hall Junior School
                Matthew Cox   70
                Ricky Malone   70
                Liam Galloway   70
                Jennie Mangles   71
                Katie Schroder   71
                Gary Charlesworth   71
                Owen Thomas   72
                Hannah Kelsall   72
                Vanessa Mills   73
                Daniel Needham   73
                Lyndsay Scott   74
                Josh Tye   74
                Lucy Williams   75
                Michael Ward   75
                Laura Burton   76
                Blue Mullins   76
                Jessica Firth   77
                Bronwyn Thomas   77
                Rachel McCabe   78
                Joe Kirk   78
                Craig Allen   79
                Rachel Mangles   79
                Melissa Brown   80
                Callam Riley   80
                Tessa White   81
                Ryan Hicks   81
                Hayley Parker   81
                Emma Wear   82
                Eethan Parks   82
                Samantha Rendi   82
                Megan Gomersall   83
                Jacob Hamshaw   84
                Emma Shaw & Toni Bellis   84
                Samantha Mullins   84
                Abby Smith   85

Thomas Thompson	85
Victoria Walker	86
Milly Mullins	86
Jennie Bower	87

Rudston Preparatory School

Luke Rhodes	87
Ben Daly	88
Ben Booth	88
Camilla Morte	89
Emma R Taylor	90
Alexander Allt	91
Hardeep Hothi	91
Thomas Pike	92
Amber Beardshall	92
Emma Taylor	93
Charlotte Furniss	94
Christian Robinson	94
Michael Akhavan Hezaveh	95
Callum Faulkner	96
Matthew Woods	96
Simon Parkin	97

Trinity Croft CE Primary School

Craig Johnson	97
Kelly Freemantle	98
Leanne Longden	98
Andrew Auty	99
Stacie Lee	99
Lisa-Marie Greaves	100

Wath Victoria J&I School

James McCarthy & Sam Holmes	100
Chloe Mitchell & Daniel Hartshorn	100
Kelly Nunn & Catherine Spencer	101
Chloe Usher & Jodie Hayselden	101
Joshua Harrison & Joe-Elliott Hobson	102
Ashleigh Turner & Megan Soame	102

The Poems

PIRATE SHIP

The pirates sailed to a treasure island.
The wind blows the sails.
The sails cut through the air
Taking the boat with them.
Hitting the waves, water splashes up on deck.
The wind waving the skull and cross bones flag.

Dark sky, black clouds, thundering.
Lightning flashes. Oh no!
The winds get stronger.
The waves crashing against the ship.
The ship rocking side to side.
Pirates cold and wet.
Go down to the cabins to get warm and dry.
All squashed together in their little rooms.
The day goes by. They fall asleep.
Suddenly they snore.
'Will you shut up!'

Morning came. They all woke up.
Went on deck and saw Treasure Island.
Jumped in the rowing boat and rowed.
Looked on the map.
Followed the route to the cross.
Started digging for the treasure chest.
'Hip hip hooray we've found it!'
Take it on board. Sail back home.
Rich for the rest of their lives.

Amy Walker, Christopher Flanagan (10)
& Janine Oldham (11)
Abbey School

THE TREASURE

We saw a tree full of apples.
We had a picnic on the beach.
We dug to make some sandcastles
And saw a treasure box.
We opened the treasure box.
There was a crown some rings and money
They were shiny and beautiful.
We saw some pirates coming to steal our treasure.
We went on a boat with our treasure
The pirates followed us.
The boat was rocking.
The water got higher and higher.
We were scared.
We made it back to the beach.
The pirate's boat sank.
We shared the treasure
And gave some to charity.

Kirsty Wilkinson, Lily Todd, Rebecca Marsden (10)
& Andrew Dalby (11)
Abbey School

TREASURE

Hidden in the sand.
Down in the deep, deep water.
Gold and silver, jewels and coins.
Necklaces and rings, bracelets.
All sorts of things.
Lost in a battle between two pirates ships of old.
Cannons blasting, fighting sword to sword.
Guarded by the fishes, crabs and seahorses.
Many pirates have searched in caves and under the sea.
But none have prevailed and the treasure lies safe
beneath the ocean blue.
Still waiting for someone to find its secret place.

Daniel Kelly (10) Jordan Leary & Jasmine Shah (11)
Abbey School

LOST LOVE

A man stands in a lonely park,
And the wind carrying his heart far across seas,
Thinking about his love that is lost forever,
Wondering if he has enough passion to last him all his life,
Looks up to the sky and sees a familiar face from when he had found
love,
He sags down into a hobo with no ambition.

Then as he gathers all his strength,
Stands up and stares at the sky,
Hoping to retrieve some of his heart,
Jumps to grab it and yells with anger,
For it was Valentine's Day.
Therefore a day of love.

And as he stumbles out,
He notices his lost love on a bench nearby,
Suddenly looks up and sees him,
Gradually walks towards him smiling,
And then finally he makes out his heart in the sky.

Sarah Billard (10)
Blackburn Primary School

MAKING AUTUMN

Take some scarlet berries, bright orange pumpkins
and some crunchy nuts.
Add some golden, crispy leaves
and a pinch of shiny, brown conkers.
Stir it all up for three months.
Decorate it with a glittery, shiny, silver web!
You have made autumn!

Bethany Woolston (8)
Blackburn Primary School

BEAUTIFUL SOUNDS, IRRITATING SOUNDS

Beautiful Sounds

I love the birds singing in a morning.
I like the sound of the motorway.
The sound of the seagulls in the air.
The thing that I like best is when people
cheer at a football match.

Irritating Sounds

I hate it when my brother shouts at me.
I dislike it when I get woken up at 7.30am.
I also hate it when my dog barks.
I hate the sound when people drop their pencils.

Joshua Harrison (9)
Blackburn Primary School

MY LITTLE TEDDY

His name is Sizzle,
He's red, he's cute,
He looks very hot,
But I wish he wasn't always mute,
His black button nose shines in the sun,
I wish he could get up and run,
He feels like a baby's skin,
His fur isn't at all like a pin,
His skin is fine,
Guess what? He's mine!

Chloe Naylor (9)
Blackburn Primary School

PLEASANT SOUNDS, UNPLEASANT SOUNDS

Pleasant Sounds

Wonderful music played by my flute teacher,
Stunning singers on the TV,
Marvellous music played on instruments,
The beautiful sound of birds singing,
The happy sound of cats purring.

Unpleasant Sounds

Annoying people messing with instruments,
The dreadful alarm clock waking me up,
The awful sound of people scratching the blackboard,
The terrible sound of the motorway,
The horrid sound of a bee buzzing in my ear.

Rebecca Andrews (10)
Blackburn Primary School

MAKING AUTUMN

Take some . . .
golden leaves,
add some wispy mist,
and some fading golden flowers.
Add a . . .
dash of bronze acorns and some ripe red berries.
Mix it all up and let it cook for three months.
Decorate it with . . .
some dark evenings and spiky green conkers,
and you have made autumn.

Billy Utley (8)
Blackburn Primary School

HOW TO MAKE AUTUMN

Take some spiky conkers,
Orange pumpkins and a dash of harvest festivals.
Add a little pinch of scarlet berries
And a cupful of rainy weather.
Mix it with crunchy leaves
And lovely golden acorns.
Then decorate it with misty grey clouds.
You have made autumn!

Eleanor K Sharpe (8)
Blackburn Primary School

WIND

Howling and hissing, the wind blew by.
Steadily through the midnight sky.
As it whispers to the trees,
They wave back in the northerly breeze.
It's so cold it makes me shiver,
And my teeth and bottom lip quiver.
Out of all the winds that I hate most,
It's when my dad's been eating beans on toast!

Victoria Strawson (11)
Blackburn Primary School

WONKY DONKEY

I knew a little donkey
Whose legs were really wonky
He wobbled around
And fell on the ground
That poor little wonky donkey.

Harly Eames (11)
Blackburn Primary School

HOW TO MAKE AUTUMN

Take some crispy golden leaves
that have fallen from the tree,
ripe acorns and scarlet berries.
Add a spoonful of spiky conkers,
a dash of crackly nuts,
a pinch of dying, fading flowers,
then stir it up.
Decorate it with a cupful of mist and white-grey sky.
You have made autumn.

Corissa Woodhouse (8)
Blackburn Primary School

MYSTIC MOONLIGHT

Mystic moonlight,
why do you shine so bright?
I like to watch you sparkle and shine,
sometimes I wish that you were all mine,
when the sun goes to bed you come out to play
and I really like to watch you shine in every way,
although you are big and bright,
you thrill me with your mystic light.

Jamie Marples (9)
Blackburn Primary School

TEXT-A-HOLIC

They're always on their mobile phones,
They push and press away,
They think it's great to text their mates,
All the bloomin' day.

Kirsty Nicholls (10)
Blackburn Primary School

NIGHT-TIME

As the long day eventually comes to an end
And that huge black sheet is placed in the sky
All that is to be seen is pitch-black silhouettes
And little glimmers of light from the little houses
That stand in the darkness of the night
As those horrible shadows creep up the wall and jump out
whenever they want
Just to scare you but don't succeed.
Then it's time for you to pop off to bed
And rest your sleepy head
When the dawn sneaks up on you
As if by magic the black sheet has been removed
And the blue sky's awoken from its sleep.

Helen Wright (11)
Blackburn Primary School

MY CAT!

My cat Sylvester is a funny little thing,
He runs around the room with a ball of string,
He likes to eat a little pink prawn,
When he's tired he gives a big yawn.
He's black and white with a little pink nose,
With very sharp claws at the end of his toes.
When he's outside he catches a mouse,
Then he tries to bring it in the house.
He's so cute and really sweet,
He's the nicest cat you'd ever meet.

Victoria Halliwell (11)
Blackburn Primary School

HAPPINESS AND ANGER

Happiness

Happiness is dark blue.
It smells like strawberry.
Happiness tastes like apples.
It sounds like love.
Happiness feels like fresh
It lives inside us.

Anger

Anger is constant red.
It smells like oranges.
Anger tastes like raw meat.
It sounds like hate.
Anger feels painful.
It lives locked up inside us.

Daniel Evans (10)
Blackburn Primary School

BRUSSELS SPROUTS

I would fight a world class boxer,
I would bungee-jump from high,
I would jump out of a jumbo jet
And glide down through the sky.
I would swim in a river with man,
Eating piranhas or a shark infested sea,
But there is no way I will
eat Brussels sprouts when
my mum gives me them for
my tea!

Anna Hardman (11)
Blackburn Primary School

HAPPINESS AND DEATH

Happiness

Happiness is rose-pink.
It smells like incense.
Happiness tastes like freshly-baked pie,
It sounds like a soft, sweet hummingbird.
It feels like a soft, furry animal,
Happiness lives in a kind, loving heart.

Death

Death is dark green
It smells like rotten meat.
Death tastes like rotten food,
It sounds like the howl of a wolf.
It feels like ice, no sound, no breath.
Death lives in a place unknown.

Jasmine Smith (10)
Blackburn Primary School

ANGER AND DISEASE

Anger

Anger is pitch-black
It smells like scolding coal,
Anger tastes like metal warming up at top speed,
It sounds like a steaming kettle,
Anger feels like a flaming stick through your heart,
It lives in the depths of underground.

Disease

Disease is murky green,
It smells like sewerage water,
It tastes like gooey slime,
Disease sounds like foghorns blowing,
Disease feels like wasps stinging you,
It lives inside you waiting to lash out.

Drew Walker (10)
Blackburn Primary School

HAPPINESS AND SADNESS

Happiness

Happiness is rose-ed
It smells like strawberries
Happiness tastes like apples
It sounds like love
It feels like home
Happiness lives in people's hearts.

Sadness

Sadness is dark blue
It smells like sky grey
Sadness tastes like grass
It sounds like somebody crying
It feels like somebody cold
Sadness lives outside in the wind.

Katherine Elliott (10)
Blackburn Primary School

SCHOOL!

I like school, I like school,
But most people say
The teachers are
Cruel!
Maths is great it can be
Your best mate,
You can play
With numbers
And for dinner you can
Have cucumbers,
As well as a sausage,
Chips or mash.
Then there's dessert which
Goes in a flash.
The day's nearly up,
Although there's PE.
We swing on the ropes
Like monkeys
in a tree.
You've done your work,
You've done it clear
The bell is ringing,
Home time's here.

Michaela Edwards (11)
Blackburn Primary School

WHO LIVES HERE?

In the distance on top of a hill,
There is a large narrow house stood very still.
This house that you see is different from the rest,
A tall spindly tree houses a crows nest.
If you look very carefully you will see who lives there,
A very old woman with thin black hair.

Nobody visits here except her black cat,
From the edge of her garden I can see a black hat.
Peering through the window I can see lots of dust,
On the side sits a plate with an old bread crust.
A thin little mouse scurries on the ground,
When I look up cobwebs hang around.

Sat in a corner the old woman strokes a black cat,
Her feet swinging over a threadbare mat.
The cloak that she wears is all tattered and torn,
Her thin pointed hat is crumpled and worn.
She has a long bony face and a pointed nose,
As she rocks in her chair she twitches her toes.

As I begin to walk down the path and look to the sky,
I notice big black clouds hovering by.
I run down the steep hill as fast as I am able,
Until I get in my house to my dinner on the table.
Can you guess who the old woman can be?
Who lives alone on the hill with a large spindly tree.

Laura Kershaw (10)
Blackburn Primary School

How To Make Autumn

Take some bright orange pumpkins,
take a peck of fluffy white seeds
and a silvery web.
Add a red flame from a bonfire
and a dark misty night.
Stir well.
Decorate it with some grey clouds
and a yellow sun.
You have made autumn.

Bethany Cudworth (7)
Blackburn Primary School

How To Make Autumn

Take a dash of golden conkers,
some smoky bonfires and orange pumpkins.
Add a pinch of crunchy vegetables and fading flowers.
Stir it up.
Decorate it with a dash of misty mornings
and dark evenings.
You have made autumn!

Lewis Hoden (8)
Blackburn Primary School

Lizzy

There was a young girl called Lizzy
Who liked things that were extremely fizzy
People told her to stop
But one day she went *pop!*
And that was the end of young Lizzy.

Faye Ducker (10)
Blackburn Primary School

MY MUM

Mum got ill in her tired, tired bed.
She went to see the doctor and he said,
'Go to the hospital to find a bed.'
Got to the massive white-walled hospital.
Oh no got bellspalsy caused by stress.
She could not have been at her very best.

Mum stayed in overnight,
That didn't half give me a fright.
All my fault, felt dreadful and bad.
I took all the blame.

I went home all sad and sorry.
Horror-struck and full of worry,
I laid on my bed, couldn't sleep,
Just stayed up with Dad.

Lucy Goffin (10)
Brinsworth Manor Junior School

CLIMBING FEAR

Climbing up, up, up, clanging
Terrified, as I got higher.
When I hit the top it made a bang
I was horrified, petrified.

I was sliding, sliding down the slippery, slippery rooftop.
It was like sliding on black oil
I slid down and fell off.

When I hit the ground it was like a cannon ball
Had hit the sea.
I got home and watched TV.

Reece Garnham (9)
Brinsworth Manor Junior School

BREAKING MY COLLAR BONE

I was at Emma's party
When I was nine
We were pinning the tail on the donkey
And I did fine.

I went in the lounge with the others
We played with a miniature ball
It was then when I tripped
And took the breaking fall.

The party ended
Then began my fear
I couldn't get up
The agony was here.

My mum came to pick me up
She took me in the car
Over bumpy potholes
And roads made of tar.

She took me to the hospital
I had to have an X-ray
They took me in a funny room
And on a bed I lay.

The nurse came to tell me what I'd done
Said the nurse 'You've broken your collar bone
Put this sling on
Then you can go home.'

Jessica Bailey (10)
Brinsworth Manor Junior School

THE ROLLER COASTER

As I board the roller coaster
The fans heat up, I feel like a toaster
It starts moving down the track
The wheels start spinning I look back.

What's this, let me see?
Over a swamp, what's to be?
This is the bit I did fear
A squeaky noise I did hear.

I wish that I was at home
Then we all started to groan
Suddenly this dreaded thing halts
I was scared worried, was it my fault?

As I start to feel dread
It spins around my confused head
Suddenly it starts to fly
As relieved, I give a sigh.

As I get off
I struggle and cough
I felt light and dizzy
I was untroubled, fizzy.

Fear comes naturally
It comes with certain things
Roller coasters, scary rides
Fear all of these will bring.

Natalia Downing (9)
Brinsworth Manor Junior School

PARROT TROUBLE

I came home at half-past three,
My cousin Leanne was looking after me.
She demanded to get my parrot out,
I said *'No!'* she replied *'I'll scream* and *shout!'*

I got him out he flew across the room.
I gasped 'I can't catch this fool.'
I sat back down to catch my breath,
All of a sudden something flew on my head.

I yelled *'What's that on my head?'*
She whispered softly and said 'It's just your parrot having a rest,'
We tried and tried but wouldn't come off,
My cousin got the scissors and merely said
'We'll have to cut your hair off.'

I was burning up like I was on fire,
I said 'You're joking' she said 'Never.'
My parrot shouting like he had been shot,
I said 'Give me a break and shut up.'
My mum came in and shouted at Leanne,
After two hours he finally came off.

Rebekka Kilby (9)
Brinsworth Manor Junior School

FEAR

Me and Anna playing games,
Mum is in the dining room
Then Mum comes in,
Making Anna jump.
So the fear starts
Anna knocks her knee
Into my mouth
Then teeth knocked out, oh no.

Blood dripping everywhere
Teeth on fluffy carpet
Mum trying to calm me down
Nothing seemed to work.
Anna shouting, 'Get a drink!'
Running into kitchen
Teeth bleeding, bleeding, bleeding.

Rachel Forrest (9)
Brinsworth Manor Junior School

PAINT PROBLEM

Energetic was the feeling on that night not long ago.
I felt thirsty like a well with no water in it so . . .
I got a drink thought I'd run with it
I hadn't spilled it yet
But that's not the thing I totally regret.

On the sunset carpet was midnight black paint,
I ran, knocked over the fizzing black splodge,
And the fireball looked a total state.
It was like an eclipse was going over the sun,
I felt fear when I realised what I'd done.

I started to panic and feel sad.
I knew Dad would be very mad.
As I watched the distant charcoal,
Ooze into the sunset red
Oh no our new carpet is ruined, I suddenly said.

Then Dad came down and did sound mad,
My fear was over and I was glad . . .
But about the paint I still feel sad.

Gemma Green (10)
Brinsworth Manor Junior School

STILL MATES

As I lashed out at the attacking boy, I felt self satisfied
but when I saw his bleeding jaw all my happiness went.
I felt sick, I did not feel well.
I just wanted to go to bed.

Then the teacher came.
I thought I was going to get the blame.
Just then I knew that that was bad,
I felt sorry, I felt sad.

She said 'Oh can't you see he isn't well,
Now look what you've done.
He looks like pond scum.
I told her my story and she said
'But why do that to his head?'

I said I was sorry he was still my mate.
We were going to play but it rained
So I got in a state.

Joshua Dugdale (10)
Brinsworth Manor Junior School

BOAT FEAR

Over the sea the boat crept,
Swiftly, swaying towards everlasting seas,
So then the boat slept, slept, slept,
Out of the window I fell, fell, fell,
Like a petal off a flower.

Over the sea I began to swim,
Over to the boat I gasped,
Only I wanted was to win, win, win
And to swim over to the boat.

Up some steps I began to climb
Up onto the boat I climbed
Wrapped in a towel I felt quite warm
And my life, I was extremely scared.

Adam Creaser (9)
Brinsworth Manor Junior School

A DREADFUL EXPERIENCE

That ordinary day when we went out,
On the bikes, to the woods.
Me, my brother and my dad, up the hill,
I knew that we would.

We got to the top and had a rest,
But then, the bike went.
And down, down, down, as fast as a cheetah would run.
I did not know why I was sent.

I hit a rock and clung on tight,
I was hanging on for dear life,
My dad came down very slowly
I thought I was in big strife.

My dad took hold of my hand,
He didn't half pull.
My arms ached, I thought I would die
This day now was very dull.

He rescued me, I was so relieved,
I walked up to the top of the hill.
I picked up my bike so quietly
I felt very ill.

William Doughty (10)
Brinsworth Manor Junior School

TOOTHPASTE DISASTER

As I started to put on the colourful, sticky
paste onto my spiky brush,
It fell.

It was like a tiny sticky worm
falling onto the cold, wet,
gritty road.

Like a soggy petal
slowly drifting away
from the stalk as rain
came tinkling down.

I was terrified,
the white mark would not move
off the bright blue carpet.

It got worse and worse,
the horrible mark laid
there, I couldn't bear
to look at it.

It looked like a huge
ugly monster.

When my mum saw
the mark on the new carpet,
she went red
like the colour of her bed!

Rachel Toplis (10)
Brinsworth Manor Junior School

UNTITLED

Rain falling down
soaking into the ground.
Streams coming together
making a river.
Waterfalls splashing
like a barracuda cheating its prey.
The river is mature
slow, wide and deep
like a tortoise walking on sand.
It meanders
sometimes it floods, like blood
it transports soil.
It erodes the river bank
like someone eating a Mars bar.
It meets the sea at its mouth
mixing like milk and strawberry
making a milkshake.
Then the journey is over.

Idnan Ali
Coleridge Primary School

SMOKING!

Smoking,
Within its depth,
Like inhaling death.
Lungs as black as panthers,
Tobacco leading down your throat,
Like a sparkling waterfall flowing
to its danger bed.
Throat cancer like bubbles on a volcano
You will always end up dead.
I know, that's for sure!

Hayley Bradbury
Coleridge Primary School

STRANGER DANGER!

Strangers so kind so sweet,
Really wanting to beat me.

On the street . . .
Asking me if I want a sweet.
Offering yummy yellow jelly beans,
Like animals hunting for their food.

Stranger danger, wanting me to come in,
Like a rabbit heading to its *death.*

So sweet, so nice helping me
Like teachers helping their students.

In the end I escape
Like a bird set free!

Nargis Hussain
Coleridge Primary School

DANGER OF DRUGS

Smoking damages your lungs,
Black like a very dark night.
Blocks your blood,
Like a van in a small road.
Dirty syringes can stick in older people's bodies,
Like a lion waiting to jump.
Drug tablets can cause you a road accident.
If you eat lots you could die
Like a withering flower.
Medicine from doctors needs much care.
If you eat too much you could die,
Like a wild animal.

Rafana Latif
Coleridge Primary School

HAPPY NEW YEAR

H is for happiness that everyone shares.
A is for anger that could start a war.
P is for peace that all the world would like.
P is for pleasant people who help the poor.
Y is New Year that people enjoy.

N is for nice people who share their food.
E is for excitement and energy that people
    have at New Year.
W is for wealthy people not poor but rich.

Y is for you who could make a difference.
E is for encouraging people to be strong.
A is for always caring for people in need.
R is for remembering family and people in the war
    that may have died or ill in any way.

Natalie Machen (10)
Listerdale (Dalton) J&I School

UNDER THE SEA

Under the sea
It's a wonderful place to be
There's exotic fish
Amazing coral
So make the most of it
One day it may not be there
Don't spoil it
Think what you'll do
It's one of Earth's treasures
Don't spoil that place deep down under the sea.

Joseph Allen (8)
Listerdale (Dalton) J&I School

A WINTER'S DAY

The burning red sun rises, hurts when I open my eyes
in the snow filled morning.

The grey misty sky makes the sun stand out
in the morning.

The sparkling snowflakes drift down to Earth
to join the others.

The icy fields have no golden corn
just a blanket of snow.

The bony trees have lost their green,
healthy leaves.

The stony houses seem to have shrunk
in the pure snow.

The hungry animals are hunting for food.

The cold birds are pecking for food.

The small children are happy building snowmen.

The orangy sunsets hide behind the snowy mountain.

Michael Schofield (10)
Listerdale (Dalton) J&I School

THE STORM

Clouds are dark and jagged racing quickly along the sky.
The sea is a pack of dogs that want dinner.
The waves are like sharks eating their prey.
The wind is a howling beast that tears at its food.
Rain is like rocks dropping from the dull grey sky.
The boat is tossed about like a fierce big fish.

Luke Salthouse (11)
Listerdale (Dalton) J&I School

HOPES AND WISHES

H   is for happiness which we wish for all the year.
O   is for optimism throughout the years.
P   is for peace which the world hopes for.
E   is for essential things that we need.
S   is for starvation we can stop.

A   is for anger which should be controlled.
N   is for never forgetting those who are in need.
D   is for decisions which everyone makes.

W   is for wishes which we hope will come true.
I   is for independence which we all hope for.
S   is for sadness throughout the world.
H   is for holidays which all people enjoy.
E   is for exams which we hope we will pass.
S   is for suffering which happens every day.

Georgina Spurr (11)
Listerdale (Dalton) J&I School

MY WINTER TREE

I like winter
When the snow is on the ground.
The trees are spooky
They look like witches' fingers.
The trunk is *coal-black*
So is the soil.
But I don't care because it is
Winter
            Winter
                    Winter.

Charlotte Gray (8)
Listerdale (Dalton) J&I School

DAYDREAMS

Mrs Toop thinks I'm reading
But I'm swinging in the jungle vines.
I'm fighting a hungry lion.
I'm swimming in the Atlantic Ocean.
Riding a chocolate pony.
I'm swimming with dolphins.
I'm swimming away from a shark.
Sunbathing in space.
Grading for my black belt at kick-boxing.
I'm riding a pony at midnight.
I'm interviewing S Club 7.
I'm in Hear'Say.
Never going to school again.
Having all the flowers in the world.
I'm eating sugar-free candy cane in Jamaica.
Having a chocolate swimming pool.
I'm on Who Wants To Be A Millionaire?

Ellie Gordon (8)
Listerdale (Dalton) J&I School

HIDDEN TREASURE UNDER THE SEA!

Hiding some treasure,
Under the sea, what can it be?
Is it some gold, oh what can it be?
It's a gold cup dazzling me!

Is there some more
Like a necklace or two?
Maybe there's a door,
That leads to a golden shoe.

Grace Binnie (10)
Listerdale (Dalton) J&I School

DAYDREAMS

Mrs Toop thinks I'm reading
But I'm not.
I'm buying a bright limousine in indigo.
I'm meeting S Club 7 in Hollywood,
I'm swimming in the ocean with the fish,
Maybe I'm finding treasure
Or I'm the queen in Never-Never Land.
I'm in Atomic Kitten at number one in the charts.
I'm skiing in a massive ice ring,
I'm riding a camel in Egypt,
I could be the animal queen of the world.
Baking lots of birthday cakes.
Mrs Toop thinks I'm working
But I'm not.
I'm the richest person in the world,
I'm picking the nice flowers from a meadow,
I am swimming with dolphins.

Sophie Cooke (8)
Listerdale (Dalton) J&I School

THE SEASHORE

S   piky swordfish dart among the coral,
E   xcited children play on the golden sand.
A   ngry waves crash against the jagged rocks.

L   ively dolphins play in the bubbling sea.
I   dle birds scavenge around the cliffs for food.
F   ish dart around in the deep blue sea.
E   els slither on the seabed.

Jamie Vernon (11)
Listerdale (Dalton) J&I School

HIDDEN TREASURE

Under the sea, a man said to me,
There was a box of treasure,
So big, so good, so beautiful,
I would love to have it.

I bought a swimsuit and put on,
My friend Clair gave me air for the goods,
So big, so good, so beautiful,
I would love to have it.

I dived down into the ocean,
I searched everywhere for the gold,
So big, so good, so beautiful,
I would love to have it.

I saw it I dived down and got it,
I swam to the surface and shouted, 'I've found it!'
It was so big, so good and so beautiful
It was just the best.

Rebecca Turner (9)
Listerdale (Dalton) J&I School

SEASHORE

S eals sinking to the bottom level.
E normous waves lashing against the crumbly rocks.
A ngry sharks swimming fast trying to catch their prey.
S ea horses floating behind the slimy soft seaweed.
H ammerhead sharks hunting for small or large fish.
O ctopuses looking around at the bright coloured fish.
R ed starfish crawling along the seabed.
E xcited children looking at all the different shells on the shore.

Rachelle Lawton (10)
Listerdale (Dalton) J&I School

HIDDEN TREASURE

My friends are my hidden treasure
They cheer me up when I am down
They always come and help me,
Even when I frown.

My friends are my hidden treasure
They play with me every day
They'll always pass the ball to me
And that's the way we play.

My friends are my hidden treasure
They'll pick me up when I fall down
They'll go and get the teacher
And wait till I come round.

My friends will always be near me
They'll always come to play
Where we play for hours on end
And one thing's for sure, they will always be my friends.

Christopher Bentley (9)
Listerdale (Dalton) J&I School

A WINTER'S DAY

Dazzling sunrises when night becomes day.
Misty blue sky making the sun look like a red ball.
White star shaped snowflakes tumble down to earth.
Icy fields have layers of snow on them.
Skeleton trees blow in the wind.
Glowing houses that look like a lump of snow.
Hungry animals that are looking for food.
Little birds that are migrating to Africa.
Finally the sun sets which looks like a sea of red.

William Jones (11)
Listerdale (Dalton) J&I School

A WINTER'S DAY

The silky red sun rises as my blurry eyes begin to open.
The milky-blue sky is almost invisible when the day grows old.
The calm smooth snowflakes sleepily fall and drift down.
The empty silver fields, which have a cover of ice, disappear
into the icy snow.
The white elfin trees turn to a skeleton as the nights grow long.
The warm fires in the houses are fighting away the cold air.
The sleepy animals make their bed underneath the icy snow.
The hungry birds search for a warm place with plenty of food.
The cold, playful children build a snowman from the icy snow.
The warm silky sunset disappears as the day freezes.

Jordan Rowbottom (10)
Listerdale (Dalton) J&I School

A WINTER'S DAY

The fiery-red sun rises to welcome a new day.
A milky-blue sky with wisps of cotton clouds.
Glistening, shining snowflakes fall slowly and
softly to the ground.
The snow-covered fields are bare and alone.
Skeleton trees sway in the cold morning air.
Cosy houses covered in candyfloss snow.
Hungry animals scavenging for food.
Migrating birds fly to the warm sun.
Excited children throwing icy snowballs at each other.
At last the glowing sunsets which brings the night with it.

Laura Bardsley (11)
Listerdale (Dalton) J&I School

HIDDEN TREASURE

Is it under the floorboards or under the stair?
I don't know do you know where?
My grandpa left this map for me
But it might be under the depths of the sea.

Under the seaweed in a shipwrecked boat,
And in the treasure it might have a secret note
Saying 'Dear all divers, don't worry about me,
Just sit down and have a cup of tea.
This treasure's probably been here years when you find it,
So try not to have a fit.'

When I find treasure my grandpa will be pleased
Oh yes, as happy as a swarm of bees.

Georgina Reynolds (9)
Listerdale (Dalton) J&I School

A WINTER'S DAY

The blazing, red sun rises when the winter morning comes.
A milky-blue sky is covered with cotton wool clouds.
Whirling, sparkling snowflakes are floating in the air as they
land softly on the ground.
White covered fields have a blanket of snow.
Skeleton-like trees covered with cotton snow sway gently.
Cosy, warm houses where the fire is burning.
Hibernating animals which have plenty of food.
Migrating birds fly away for the winter.
Joyful children play happily in the freezing cold.
Glowing orange sunsets end the winter's day.

Laura Parker (10)
Listerdale (Dalton) J&I School

HIDDEN TREASURES

My treasure is quite small
My treasure is multicoloured
My treasure is hidden in my room
My treasure is delicate
My treasure was a present
My treasure is alone
My treasure not many know about
My treasure can easily break
My treasure is my mood lamp.

Lewis Davenport (9)
Listerdale (Dalton) J&I School

SEA LIFE

S eals are swimming and diving and wobbling ashore.
E ndangered manatee with a curling clown nose.
A nemones waving as currents pass by.

L impets sticking on rocks and scuttling in pools.
I dle birds, like herring gulls, scavenge in dumps.
F ishing cables floating and bumping in the bay.
E els waving and dodging in amongst the weed.

Christopher Brookes (10)
Listerdale (Dalton) J&I School

HIDDEN TREASURES UNDER THE SEA

Hidden treasures under the sea,
Dive down what can you see,
Underwater you seek,
Inside a box, take a peek.

Open it up different things,
Gold diamonds silver rings,
Red rubies lots of gold,
Necklaces that I hold.

Katie Palethorpe (10)
Listerdale (Dalton) J&I School

THE ROBIN

The robin sits on the branch of a tree,
All around it's as cold as can be,
He's such a lovely sight to see,
Covered in snow on the edge of that tree.
So stop to admire him when you pass by
Yet do not disturb him or away he will fly,
Then the children around will all ask why
The robin's not there when they pass by.

Philippa Spencer (9)
Listerdale (Dalton) J&I School

SEA LIFE

S   cuttling crabs digging into the wet, soggy sand.
E   xcited, giddy children paddling in the waving sea.
A   ngry circling waves splashing on shining shells.

L   ively dolphins jumping happily over the huge waves.
I   dle birds scavenging for scared crabs in the drying sand.
F   loating driftwood banging against the rough rocks.
E   lectric eels slithering through the slimy seaweed.

Bridey Dunkley (10)
Listerdale (Dalton) J&I School

A STORMY NIGHT

The crooked rain bounced on to the narrow pavement.
The tangling trees stood out in the pitch night.
The wind was a howling vicious beast.
The thunder roared like a tiger in pain.
The lightning blinded my sea blue eyes.
The moon looked like a circular evil beam.
I hid behind my shielding window
And waited for the storm to pass.

Gareth Hall (11)
Listerdale (Dalton) J&I School

SHARING

S   is for starvation, when many people need food.
H   is for helping, those who are ill.
A   is for Afghans, who are hungry and dying.
R   is for remembering, those who have died.
I   is for illnesses, that people catch.
N   is for NSPCC who help children who need help.
G   is for giving, food to poor.

Maria Peters (10)
Listerdale (Dalton) J&I School

DAYDREAMS

Mrs Toop thinks I'm reading
But I'm playing rugby
And I'm wrestling a crocodile
And I'm a wizard making potions to cure
Animals and to make people better.

Curtis Smith (8)
Listerdale (Dalton) J&I School

HIDDEN TREASURES

Hidden treasures under the sea.
What can it be?
Silver diamonds,
Golden rings,
What can it be?

Hidden treasure under the sea,
What can it be?
Gold bracelets,
Silver necklaces,
What can it be?

Hidden treasure under the sea,
What can it be?
Shiny diamonds
Purple jewels,
What can it be?

Bryony Penn (10)
Listerdale (Dalton) J&I School

RESOLUTION

R   is for remembering the people gone by.
E   is for excitement which comes every year.
S   is for sadness for those we have lost.
O   is for opportunities that everyone has.
L   is for loneliness which the people in the streets have.
U   is for useless which no one is.
T   is for thanks which we say for fun times.
I   is for independence which everyone needs.
O   is for options that we can choose.
N   is for never forgetting the homeless.

Matthew Hulley (11)
Listerdale (Dalton) J&I School

MY HIDDEN TREASURE

My hidden treasure is very special to me.
She always listens to me.
She is special because deep inside her I know she is like a star.
She sparkles above most people and is special in every way.

My hidden treasure is a fighter,
She spoils me rotten always making me
Feel happy when I'm sad.
My hidden treasure lives in a little village.
My hidden treasure is loving and caring.

My hidden treasure always helps the sick.
She always looks for jobs to do.
She goes round with her Hoover and polish.
In the end her little figures are sparkling like the stars,
Like the star inside her.

    My hidden treasure is my *grandma!*

Jessica Royle (10)
Listerdale (Dalton) J&I School

A WINTER'S DAY

Dazzling red sunrises when the cold is around,
The milky-blue sky is empty with no clouds.
The star like snowflakes drift to the ground.
Snow covered fields have footprints here and there.
Skeletal trees sway to and fro.
Warm and cosy houses are hiding places from the cold.
The hungry animals search for their food.
The cold birds migrate for the winter.
Happy, joyful children throw snowballs at each other.
Warm orange sunsets slowly drift away.

Rebecca Summerfield (10)
Listerdale (Dalton) J&I School

HIDDEN TREASURES

At the bottom of the sea
Some treasures can be found
They can be found by anyone
Even the mayor, the fisherman
And someone from the zoo.
The treasure would be welcomed by anyone you know
Even so, the treasure I like this treasure the most
People would like the most.
While you are a baby, you don't realise this treasure or what it was for.
Now you are older you will realise what that treasure was
Your treasure is your family.
The thing that's always there.
The thing you sometimes take for granted.
With that treasure you always have a shoulder to cry on.
And surely that treasure is the best.
Yes you may be able to find that hidden treasure at the
                                    bottom of the sea.
But also remember that you can find hidden treasure in your heart.

Charlotte Scothern (10)
Listerdale (Dalton) J&I School

THE BLUE OCEAN

S   wimming whales speed through the ocean.
E   lectric eels hide in the rough rocks.
A   ngry waves bombard the huge and jagged rocks.

L   ifeboats rush into the never-ending sea.
I   dle birds scavenge on the golden beach.
F   loating driftwood rides the tall waves.
E   xcited children play on the gold sand.

Antony Sharpe (10)
Listerdale (Dalton) J&I School

WOOF! WENT THE DOG

Woof! Went the dog,
When he ran off to the park.

Woof! Went the dog
When it got dark.

Woof! Went the dog
When he was alone.

Woof! Went the dog
When he found a bone.

Woof! Went the dog
When he went back to his house.

Woof! Went the dog
When he saw a little mouse.

Woof! Went the dog
When he fell fast asleep.

Woof! Went the dog
When he was dreaming about a sheep.

Adam Roddis (8)
Listerdale (Dalton) J&I School

HIDDEN TREASURE

In the sea, deep, deep down,
Is hidden treasure right by a town.
The chest is full of rubies and rings,
Silver, gold, shiny things.

The chest is made of wood and gold,
With a silver lock never to be sold.
The key is hidden deep in a well
And the man who guards it never to tell.

Nobody has ever found the chest,
Anybody who wants to must pass a test.
If nobody finds it then it must stay there,
At the bottom of the sea, deep and bare.

Owen Jones (10)
Listerdale (Dalton) J&I School

HIDDEN TREASURE

Diving underwater into the sea,
Something sparkly and shiny,
It's glowing brightly like a star,
You can see it shining brightly,
It's hidden treasure in the sand,
In an open ancient chest,
Covered in green wavy seaweed,
Goldfish swim around it.

A fish swims around it,
Like it's guarding it,
From divers trying to find it,
The glow of gold shines,
It shines on the fish,
A grey shark appears,
The fish swim away,
Crunch! It destroys the treasure.

No more glow shining,
It's gone, all gone.
No more sparkles,
A mark of the chest,
It's all that's left,
Of treasure,
Of hidden treasure,
All the rest is gone.

Kataleya Orr (9)
Listerdale (Dalton) J&I School

DAYDREAMS

Mrs Toop thinks I'm listening
But I'm thinking I'm a scientist
Making a potion to cure the poorly people.
Now I'm a footballer I'm in team
Daydream and I scored a terrific goal.
I'm a soldier for the Navy against the USA
And my team's won.
I'm a racer in my race car and I'm in the lead
And I can see the finish line and I've won.
'Yaaaaaaa' go the fans.
Mrs Toop heard me scream and I was for it now
As Mrs Toop screamed at me.

Thomas King (8)
Listerdale (Dalton) J&I School

CHRISTMAS

C is for crazy crackers popping at a party
H is for prickly green holly dangling on a tree
R is for Prince *Rudolph* pulling on the sleigh
I   is for ivy hanging by a thread
S   is for *Santa* giving children presents.
T   is for teamwork, getting all the presents to
      boys and girls on time for *Christmas.*
M is for mistletoe underneath are boys and girls
A   is for amazing presents that lay on the ground
S   is for socks and shoes that get
            wet.

Yasmin Ahmad (8)
Listerdale (Dalton) J&I School

HIDDEN TREASURE POEM

I sit on the floor in my bedroom
Thinking of what to do
Through my window flowers bloom
I wish I was one too.

Inside the flower lay a pot of treasure
It is such a lovely pleasure
To have it there
Beside the pear.

The treasure is hidden in the flower
Because the flower will never die
The birds probably think it is sour
But I think it is as cute as pie.

Laura Clewes (9)
Listerdale (Dalton) J&I School

HIDDEN TREASURES

My family are my hidden treasures
My sister, my mum and dad,
They take me out on fun day trips,
But we stay at home when I'm bad.

My pet is my hidden treasure
A little hamster called Ellie
My mum thought she'd smell a lot
But she's not at all quite smelly.

My friends are my hidden treasures
They play with me at school.

Natalie Taylor (9)
Listerdale (Dalton) J&I School

FLOWERS

Flowers are all different colours
People like flowers and I do too.
Flowers are purple, flowers orange, flowers are yellow.
All kinds of colours and smell good too.
Big flowers, small flowers, tall flowers that you can hide
behind
Boo!
Flowers are all different colours.
I like flowers
Do you?

Lorren Clark (8)
Listerdale (Dalton) J&I School

DAYDREAMS

Mrs Toop thinks I'm listening but I'm not.
I'm driving a train in train town an imaginary place.
I'm in a chocolate pool before going on the Flying Scotsman.
Now I'm eating ice cream in the station.
Oh no I have spilt ink on my work.

Wesley Wharmsby (8)
Listerdale (Dalton) J&I School

THE SUN

The sun is bright, the sun is shiny.
The flowers shine and sparkle in the sun.
The flowers look beautiful in the sun, they sparkle all day.
Children play in the sun, they eat ice cream all day.
The sun sparkles all day.

Sabah Ali (9)
Listerdale (Dalton) J&I School

DAYDREAMS

Mrs Toop thinks I'm reading
But I'm not.
I've got £200,000 pounds.
I buy a turquoise limousine,
I am a secret agent on a mission,
I have lots of chocolate kittens and puppies,
I'm going to the mall to buy a sparkly silk dress.
Mrs Toop thinks I'm listening
But I'm not.
I'm in the pool, it's got chocolate water,
My TV only has 'The Simpsons' on it,
Oh bother! I've got my work ruined.

Lucy Brookes (8)
Listerdale (Dalton) J&I School

DAYDREAMS

Mrs Toop thinks I'm reading
But I'm ice skating on fragile ice.
I'm wrestling, I'm punching hard.
I'm playing football with the champ.
I'm fighting in the First World War.
Now I'm fighting sharks in the deep ocean,
But now I'm a robber stealing things
Or exploring a dark cave in the sea.
Now I'm a Viking invading England,
But now I'm a Martian invading space
Or shooting at massive pigeons with my gun.

Joseph Stanley (8)
Listerdale (Dalton) J&I School

DAYDREAMS

Mrs Toop thinks I'm listening but
I'm in the ice-age fighting a deadly beast
called the woolly rhino
and the underwater beast.
No I'm not I'm zombie fighting on a stage
No I'm not I'm a footballer and I have just won the World Cup.
Maybe not I'm in a room full of ice crème and money
I'm a secret agent jumping on tall buildings and spying on people.

Fabian Agana (8)
Listerdale (Dalton) J&I School

DAYDREAMS

Mrs Toop thinks I'm reading
But I am really dreaming.
Of sharks snapping fish down
And swordfish having a fight.
Snorkels swimming around the sea and
Making funny twirls.
People sitting on the beach,
Me fishing on the bank side watching fish dive.

Samuel Abbotts (8)
Listerdale (Dalton) J&I School

A WINTER'S DAY

Dazzling red sunrises when night becomes day.
The milky-blue sky is shaded by mist.
Sparkling snowflakes drift down to the ground.
Snowy blanket-covered fields have footsteps every now and again.
Skeletal trees sway gently in the wind.

Cold houses are soon made warm by their blazing fire.
Hibernating animals are all nice and cosy while they sleep,
Migrating birds fly to the warm places of the world.
Excited children sledge down the hills.
The golden sunsets tell people night is awake.

Victoria Willcock (10)
Listerdale (Dalton) J&I School

DAYDREAMS

Mrs Toop thinks I'm listening
But actually I'm swimming in money.
Fighting, large, runny chocolate monsters,
I'm the ruler of the world,
The strongest person in the world,
Eating a year's worth of sweets
In a chocolate swimming pool,
on Mars fighting big, green, slimy Martians.

Ben Marshall (8)
Listerdale (Dalton) J&I School

HIDDEN TREASURE

Hidden treasure all around
Up in hills or on the ground
In your heart and your head
Maybe in your bed.
My treasure could be cute and small
My treasure could be rough and tall
Hidden treasure all around
Up in hills or on the ground.

Jonathan Wharmsby (9)
Listerdale (Dalton) J&I School

RIDDLE OF THE SEA

My first is in cod
and also in crab.

My second in lobster
and never in dab.

My third and my sixth
are both found in roach.

My fourth is in salmon
so good to poach.

My fifth is in eel
but never in conger.

My seventh and eighth
the same, only longer.

My ninth is in fish
and fine finny flocks.

My whole is a living collection of rocks.

Jessica Skitt (8)
Dearne Carrfield Primary School

BROTHERS

B   en is my brother and he drives me crazy,
R   unning around never being lazy.
O   n and on he goes thinking he's a Power Ranger,
T   hroughout the day he pretends he's in danger.
H   e's four years old and very funny,
E   verybody loves him because he's as cute as a bunny.
R   eally everyone should have *one!*

Emily Morris (8)
Dearne Carrfield Primary School

PLAYSTATION

My PlayStation and I
Are wonderful friends
It never tells me that
Our play has to end.
It keeps me occupied
When I am bored
And when I am finished,
Its memory is stored.

My homework is done
It's off upstairs at a very fast run.
But don't get confused
And don't get this wrong,
PlayStation games are not just fun
It also teaches me while playing
It's a lot of fun.

John Hunt (8)
Dearne Carrfield Primary School

MY BEDROOM

The colour of my carpet is blue,
So are my curtains too.
I have a large cabin bed,
Where at night I lay my head.
On my ceiling there's some stars
And on my shelf there are lots of cars.
I have posters on my wall
And some of them are of Darth Maul.
My favourite toys
Are ones made for boys.

Daniel Johnson (8)
Dearne Carrfield Primary School

MY HAMSTER

My hamster is called Silky,
But most of the time I call her Stinky,
My hamster is a female,
She tries to escape - but unfortunately fails.
Silky bites on the cage when she wants to come out,
My mum will flick her nose and shout,
With this Silky will shiver with fright,
She will hide under her bedding till she's out of sight.
Silky can tell who people are,
She can tell whether they're near or far.
If there is any sound,
She will lift her head up from the ground.
Silky will go anywhere for food,
Her face shows her every mood,
She's the second hamster I've had,
Silky is cheeky and also mad.
I've told you about my friendly pet
And how she can get quite upset,
Silky is my only pet
And she is the best yet!

Rebecca Dalby (9)
Dearne Carrfield Primary School

MY SISTER DARCY

My sister Darcy is smaller than me
And I can lift her up quite easily.
She can't lift me
She's tried and tried,
I must have something heavy inside.

Cody Mellor (7)
Dearne Carrfield Primary School

OUR REAL TEACHERS

Mrs French teaches maths
The mystery of her is her eye.
She sees boys who couldn't lie.
There's Mr Scratch he teaches song,
He has a secret girlfriend
And I think he's been away a bit too long.
Now Principle Trickery he's a smart chap
He walks around wearing a deep black cap.
He can make you work hard with one sharp clap
How do I know this you may ask?
It's a secret I keep buried in my desk
To find the answer that you seek,
Go around the school and find my seat.

James Dunn (9)
Dearne Carrfield Primary School

BROTHERS

My brothers, they are a pain
They drive me so insane.
They fight over the computer
And they say they will be good in future.
They think they are so cool
But they know I am not a fool.
They like to stay out late
With their best mates.
They like to play football
But never pays for a phone call.
Before they go to bed,
They always like to be fed.

Laura Green (10)
Dearne Carrfield Primary School

MY BEST FRIEND

My dog Jack
Is nearly all black.
With a white chest
That I like best.

When I say walk
He almost talks.
He gets really excited
And highly delighted.

I teach him to do tricks
Like jumping over sticks
He loves to go on holiday
And likes to swim in the sea
He digs deep holes on the beach
And buries me so deep.
I love my furry friend.

Liam Highfield (8)
Dearne Carrfield Primary School

THE MUMMIES

A shadeless sun beat hazily down.
Upon the sandy sunkissed ground.
Hills and sand dunes temples comb
The only place mummies loom.

Passengers, scallywags, secret and dark
Pyramids a mummy's favourite park.
Places to play hide-and-seek.
Too scary by even to speak.

Gold and jewels treasure a fold
Lay around or so I'm told.
Guarded by the mummy's curse
I would wish I had some in my purse.

Dominic Williamson (8)
Dearne Carrfield Primary School

MY BEST FRIEND TIGER

My best friend Tiger is a fluffy ginger cat
He sits licking his paws on the kitchen mat.
He runs round the garden playing in the sun,
Chasing the butterflies having so much fun.
Tiger lays with me when I go to bed.
He curls up in a ball and purrs when I stroke his head.
I love Tiger and he loves me,
He's my best friend don't you agree?

Emma Cowley (8)
Dearne Carrfield Primary School

REBECCA

R   ose red cheeks that is me,
E   at and drinking as I please,
B   ecky's my nickname Beck also,
E   ating healthy eating well,
C   ome to my house run, run, run, don't make me wait,
    come, come, come, come.
C   all me Beck, Becky but whatever you do don't call me Rebecca!
A   lmost my poem is finished, hope you like it Byeeeeee.

Rebecca Taylor (8)
Dearne Carrfield Primary School

MY FAMILY

Mum
My mum is my future, my mum is my cook.
Just before bedtime she reads me a book.
The day I was born was the day I met her.
When I am sick she gives me some medicine to help me get better.
My mum is the greatest, she is the best
She's the world's greatest
Mum in the whole wide west.

Dad
My dad is an art genius, my dad is a computer freak,
When he goes to the toilet 'phew what a reek'
He loves pepperoni pizza with mushrooms and cheese.
He loves The Simpsons, 'So pass the remote please.'
When the dog is naughty he whacks it with a pillow.
But the thing he wants for his birthday is an armadillo.
He is my dad, yes he is my dad.
He buys me toys that makes me glad.

Jason
Jason was my brother he had a case of cancer,
Under that bald head he was the best baby dancer.
He was a fighting brave Star Wars cadet,
And he was the best brother I ever met.
He is an angel now and having some fun,
Messing up the clouds and shooting rainbows with his toy gun.
That day he died he broke my heart,
But I still love him, even though we're apart.

Chappie
Chappie is my dog, he bites me a lot,
If he was taken we would have a girl one named Dot.
He is now allowed outside where he gets mucky,
He is a wonderful playful puppy.

His favourite toy is a mouse in cheese,
We give him a bath so he won't get fleas.
I love my dog Chappie and play with him every day,
He is now part of my family and that's the way it will stay.

Emily Tarff (8)
Dearne Carrfield Primary School

LEEDS UNITED

Leeds United are the best,
They have passed every test.
Viduka, Mills and Smithy too
Quickly scored and didn't know what to do.
Nigel Martyn had a goal kick
Knocked Mills absolutely sick.

Nigel Martyn let the ball roll,
And the other side scored a goal.
Now *Leeds* are one-nil down,
Martyn feels like a clown.
He stands and hangs his head in shame,
I bet he won't do that again.

The ball comes and he's prepared,
The man with the ball is very scared.
The crowd were shouting 'Get stuck in
Because we want you to win!'

Now the game is near the end,
Martyn would not have a friend.
Martyn let the ball roll,
Viduka scored a fantastic goal
What a match I must admit
At least I'm good and fit.

Patrick Desbrough & Brandon Crook (9)
Dearne Carrfield Primary School

BROWNIE GUIDE FOOTPATH

I'm going on a journey
Down the Brownie Guide footpath
There's bound to be some hard work,
But I'm sure I'll have a laugh.

I've got to be wide awake
Not walk round in a dream
To find lots of interesting important things
To be part of a team.

I've got to keep myself healthy
Know my body parts and things they do.
Keeping fit, swimming, skipping,
Eat healthy fruit and vegetables too.

I've got to try to do my best
In everything I do
Even when the job seems hard
And I haven't got a clue.

I've got to try to make things
Like this poem that I have wrote
But making toys and decorations
Will always get my vote.

I've got to be friendly
With people in this land
To get to know other Brownies
Over the sea and over the land.

I have to have fun out of doors
Taking a look at all things wild
Looking at birds, trees and flowers,
I'm just glad the weather's mild.
I know it sounds like a long walk,
But remember it's a footpath not a mile.

Lauren Marsh (9)
Dearne Carrfield Primary School

MY BROTHER RYAN

My brother Ryan looked cute in his cot
But when he got poorly, he always got hot,
And I said, *'Ryan!'*

He liked to play with his toys
Like his piano, his trains and his army boys
And I said, *'Ryan!'*

He looked at his books and other things too
He played hide-and-seek and he shouted, 'Boo.'
And I said, *'Ryan!'*

And now that he's older he plays on his bike
He goes so fast it makes me go *Yike!*
And I said, *'Ryan!'*

When he gets older maybe he'll tell
What makes me so mad and makes me yell
And I said, *'Ryan!'*

Hannah King (9)
Dearne Carrfield Primary School

DANIEL

D is for Daniel, my little baby brother.
A is for active, he bounces like no other.
N is for naughty which he never is.
I is for important that he is to me.
E is for eating, he never seems to stop.
L is for laughing, he does that a lot.

Katrina Pugh (8)
Dearne Carrfield Primary School

THE BRIGHT RAINBOW

R ainbows are colourful and bright
A methyst is one of those that make it a sight.
I vy is used to make it nice.
N avy is a very nice colour.
B lue is a boy's favourite.
O range is juicy and sweet.
W hite is like silver.

Brittany Beighton (7)
Dearne Goldthorpe Primary School

JUNGLE

J ungles have treasure in different places
U nder the spooky trees
N ext to where the monkeys sleep
G old and rubies
L ooking at me
E lephants take all the treasure.

Katie Fletcher (7)
Dearne Goldthorpe Primary School

MY HAUNTING DREAM

Clocks chiming at 13 o'clock,
Then I heard an eerie knock.
Screams of horror from the hall,
Small creatures started to crawl.
I looked in there to have a peep
And then suddenly with a leap,
I ran off down the hall,
Then tripped over a big eyeball.
As it winked up at me,
I trembled with fear and started to wee.
My pants were soaking and found it hard to run
And with a bump I ran into Mum.
I woke up with a shock
And Mum said 'What's up, cock?'
It woke me with a jump,
Then my heart started to pump.
Ever since that morning,
It always gave me a warning.
I go to bed at night
And it still gives me a little fright.

Georgina Bentham (11)
Dearne Goldthorpe Primary School

HAUNTED HOUSE

H   aunted house with a monster
O   h, so big and strong
U   nder the floorboards
S   queaky and old, that's where the
E   meralds are kept.

Lewis Freeman (9)
Dearne Goldthorpe Primary School

PRECIOUS TREASURE

My treasures, these are
My precious teddy, so old I love it so much.
My precious model so old, it's the best thing I've got.
My wonderful rabbit teddy I love and it's so big.
I love all my pets so soft.
My pets that are dead are my treasure forever.
Emerald is my birthstone, so green, so nice.
My family I can keep is my treasure forever and ever.
My dog is my treasure, Cindy is her name, my aunt gave her to me.
My mouse teddy of colours is my treasure too.
All my toys are my treasures.
My Beanies are my best treasure of all
They are so pretty and small.
That's all.

Jessica Bywater (8)
Dearne Goldthorpe Primary School

PLUG HOLE DIVING SPIDERS

Plug hole diving spiders with their little tiny feet
Plug hole diving spiders they have nowhere else to sleep.
Plug hole diving spiders in the corner of my eye
Plug hole diving spiders waiting for a fly.
Plug hole diving spiders no time to make a web.
Plug hole diving spiders use a plug hole for a bed.
Plug hole diving spiders they appear from down the drain.
Plug hole diving spiders they disappear down there again.

Sadie O'Connor (10)
Dearne Goldthorpe Primary School

THE JUNGLE HOUSE

H aunted house is in the jungle
A nd a peaceful jungle it is
U nder the haunted house there is a ghost
N ext to a cupboard I found some
T reasure and
E meralds and gold were shining in my face
D iamonds, I was rich! Are you?

H aunted ghost in the house, I ran
O ut like thunder.
U nderneath the haunted house the
S cary ghost lives.
E very time you go there, you never come back.

Christopher Timmins (8)
Dearne Goldthorpe Primary School

HIDDEN TREASURES

He's worn from years of loving.
Every night I go and hug him.
He's really precious to me and all of my family
And he's called Little Snowy.
I've had him for years and years
And he's got pretty tatty ears.
He is really old
And he could never be sold
Because he's my very own little teddy.

Thomas Jane (9)
Dearne Goldthorpe Primary School

LIFE ON MARS

Alien invasion! Alien invasion!
The school stayed silent.
Not even a phone rang.
Then panic!

Pupils raced along corridors.
Teachers shouted, 'Stop!'
Children chanted,
'It's the men from Mars.'
Teachers laughed.
The delivery of the chocolate
Was unleashed.

Alison Fletcher (10)
Dearne Goldthorpe Primary School

DONUT TREASURE

Here are the donuts standing on the ground
They are brown and go round and round.
When I have donuts and tea,
It always makes me feel like everything's me.
The last day of my holiday in the car seat.
I went to the seaside, what could I see?
A very shiny donut just ready to eat
And when I got home there were donuts everywhere.
So we ate them all.
At the end we grew very tall,
And after we had burped we shrank back small.

Kirsty Suchacki (7)
Dearne Goldthorpe Primary School

BRADLEY'S POEM

There was something in front of me.
It was a feather and controlled the weather.
I was amazed that it had such a blaze!
I made the weather rain.
Then in a slight voice the feather said the rain was going
to stop so I made it rain again.
It was midnight but you could see the moonlight.
Now I know the feather is a treasure.
It had little pearls like curls.
Actually they did curl
And the top pieces were gold just like the world.

Bradley Whiteman (8)
Dearne Goldthorpe Primary School

GHOST'S TREASURE

I love haunted houses.
They are spooky and crooked.
They are filled with pots of gold.
Aliens live at the bottom of the stairs
With a net on top of them.
Treasure is buried under the stairs.
Everybody wants it but they can't reach it.
Diamonds are in the box.
The diamonds are silver and gold.
The key is in the box and it slowly opens.
The aliens escape.

James Stevenson (8)
Dearne Goldthorpe Primary School

WALKING ON THE MOONLIT PATH

Walking on the moonlit path,
At the starry midnight hour,
Wondering where it leads to next,
Staring up at the twinkling sky.

Looking at my cold little toes,
Surrounded by growing darkness,
Dressed in a blue silk gown,
Walking on the moonlit path.

Calm running through my mind,
Suddenly I see a dim light,
It is a lovely lost star,
Walking on the moonlit path.

I think I've found what I'm looking for,
I come to a shuddering halt.
Staring up at a dim lantern,
I've been walking on a moonlit path.

Becky Jane (11)
Dearne Goldthorpe Primary School

I WANT TREASURE

T   reasure, treasure I want treasure.
R   ings and things.
E   meralds and golden strings.
A   methyst shine like a golden jewel.
S   apphire rings and wedding rings.
U   ncover all the jewels.
R   ubies and gems.
E   lizabeth our Queen has all of these things.

Bradley Grant (8)
Dearne Goldthorpe Primary School

HIDDEN TREASURE

H iding beneath hot dry sand,
I nside a chest on a desert land
D iamonds sparkle,
D ollars, there are plenty,
E nough to last us to another century, but
N obody knows where to find the entry.

T o find the treasure we need a map
R eading it may lead us into a trap.
E xactly where to find it is unknown,
A lmost leading us to another zone.
S earching and looking,
U nsure where to go
R ound the island we are shown
E veryone's looking but nobody will own,
   the hidden treasure buried alone.

Chanelle Henshaw (11)
Dearne Goldthorpe Primary School

WASHING UP

Hank goes out and drives a car
Danny plays a mean guitar
John goes out and drives a plane
And Wendy's washing up again.

Hank will get a promotion soon
Danny's tune is number one.
John is flying to Southern Spain
But Wendy's washing up again.

Natalie Beighton (11)
Dearne Goldthorpe Primary School

What Heaven Is Like

Rolling waves upon the sand,
Children playing hand-in-hand.
Clouds are floating up above,
Each one like a little dove.

Bobbing sails on the sea,
Babies giggling happily.
Adults reposing in deckchairs,
Tipping sand upon them unawares.

Now you'll see this life is grand,
Playing here beside the sand
And one day you'll join us here,
Because death is naught to fear.

Sarah Jones (11)
Dearne Goldthorpe Primary School

The Haunted House

In a haunted house on the furthest chair
Was an alien hiding treasure.
It was a misty night and the house was creepy.
All the gold was rusty and the dragon's wings were dirty.
So they couldn't fly.
A monster was snoring under the staircase with the
                                        gold that everyone wanted
But they couldn't have it.
There was gold, rubies and sapphires.

Callum Cooper (7)
Dearne Goldthorpe Primary School

THE PLUMPY PIG

There once was a plumpy pig,
As lazy as ever could be.
He laid in his bed and bumped his head
And said, 'Oh deary me!'

There once was a plumpy pig,
As lazy as ever could be.
He laid in the mud and stood on a bud
And said, 'Oh deary me!'

There once was a plumpy pig,
As lazy as ever could be.
He was so huge he ate lots of food,
Oh deary, deary me!

Zoe Iles (11)
Dearne Goldthorpe Primary School

TREASURE

Silver and sapphires are brilliant.
A locket in a treasure box.
A sword stuck like a fox.
Diamonds, topaz, ruby and jet.
Ivory is the richest stone.
Citrine is the brightest.
Pearl is the smallest.
Ruby is the middle size
And amethyst is the biggest.
I love all the stones
Because they are all bright!

Amy Kilner (7)
Dearne Goldthorpe Primary School

TRAPPED IN A DREAM

Walking in the starry night,
Upon the shimmering, silver light.
Floating higher than a kite,
Looking at the sparkling sight.

Calm rushing through my mind
As noisiness goes behind.
Something that I have to find,
As I close my dark eyes' blinds.

Things are not as they seem,
As if I'm floating on a stream.
What I'm looking for, I think I've just seen,
But now I'm trapped in a dream.

Gwen Tsang (10)
Dearne Goldthorpe Primary School

THE EARTH

The Earth, the Earth
You are mine
You are nice and you are kind.

We sit on you
All through the night,
We see the stars,
A-sparkling bright,
Up, up in the darkest sky.

You are made from land
And water,
For all God's creatures,
They will live, thank goodness.

Emma Chambers (10)
Dearne Goldthorpe Primary School

HAUNTED

H aunted house had a dead witch
A nd some treasure
U nder the treasure
N umbers of ghosts are haunting the house
T reasure is everywhere
E veryone is running away
D ragons are sleeping in the corner.

Matthew Suggett (8)
Dearne Goldthorpe Primary School

JUNGLE

J ungles are full of treasure, it's hot
U nder the ground I sold a tray of gold
N ot far away from the jewels they looked old
G old I went cold, and my eye went funny
L ittle jewels, gems, crystal, rubies, citrines
E meralds are shiny and green.

James Brice (8)
Dearne Goldthorpe Primary School

WILD LIFE

J ungle creeps and it makes me dream of sweets but I am looking for
U nusual treasure like rubies, gold nuggets, turquoise rings. It is
N ight now I hope to find some gold. The next day I went hunting,
G old, I have found it. I am rich. There were pearls and gold.
L ucky me! Then I found a parrot, it was red, yellow and blue, it was
E xciting.

James Jones (8)
Dearne Goldthorpe Primary School

GUESS

A boiling burner
A red thriller
An Earth scorcher
A skin burner
A moon reflector
A ball of gold
A spectacular scene.

Matthew Cox (10)
Lilly Hall Junior School

THE SUN - KENNING

A red thriller,
A flame thrower,
An Earth warmer,
A morning welcomer,
A moon reflector,
A suntan burner,
A sand scorcher.

Ricky Malone (10)
Lilly Hall Junior School

MORNING YARD

Sunshine, sun glow, sun bright,
make the flowers grow,
once seeds now a paradise of flowers.
Red, white, yellow, blue, green, flowers and roses,
butterflies dancing in and out of the flowers,
while busy busy bees bring honey to their queen.

Liam Galloway (8)
Lilly Hall Junior School

THE VAMPIRE'S GRAVE

It is dark and gloomy where the vampire lays.
The vampire waits for supper to come,
In three seconds the vampire rises,
It grabs you and it sticks its fangs into your neck,
Then you're dead, your body is laying on the ground.
There is blood dripping from his fangs,
The vampire laughs, has he dropped into deep black grave?

Jennie Mangles (9)
Lilly Hall Junior School

MOON

Silent silver shining moon up in our night sky,
Stood still like a giant ball that had been tossed up
and attached to our night sky.   .
Suddenly standing still it starts to fade away,
So slowly, so silently, it shimmers.
Softly, sweeping, spreading across the night sky,
It disappears.

Katie Schroder (10)
Lilly Hall Junior School

SUN

It wakes the people on Earth
It makes the Earth welcoming and warm.
It is the hottest star in our solar system.
At sunset it rests and waits for morning.
In the morning it is eager to wake us up!

Gary Charlesworth (11)
Lilly Hall Junior School

THE EGG YOLK THAT WAS RED

The egg yolk that was red
The egg yolk that was re
The egg yolk that was r
The egg yolk that was
The egg yolk that wa
The egg yolk that w
The egg yolk that
The egg yolk tha
The egg yolk th
The egg yolk t
The egg yolk
The egg yol
The egg yo
The egg y
The egg
The eg
The e
The
Th
T

Owen Thomas (9)
Lilly Hall Junior School

ANIMALS

Foxes sleep in a den
Pigs get messy in a pen.

Horses run wild in a field
Tortoises have a nice hard shield.

Monkeys swing high in trees
I don't like bumblebees.

The fly somersaults in the air
There's a grizzly hairy bear!

Shh there is a dormouse still sleeping
The rabbit is cheekily peeping.

Hannah Kelsall (10)
Lilly Hall Junior School

MY TEDDY

My teddy is cuddly,
I love my teddy.
When I am scared I cuddle him.
My mum loves teddies.
He has little clothes.
My teddy is a little teddy.
When I am asleep he sleeps with me.
    My teddy.

Vanessa Mills (9)
Lilly Hall Junior School

FOOTBALL

The blue football,
The blue, blue ball.
The blue player,
The blue man,
As fast as a football player.
As good as a football player.
As good as a Liverpool player.
Liverpool, Liverpool, are the best.

Daniel Needham (8)
Lilly Hall Junior School

BABY, BABY

Baby, baby,
So soft and sweet,
With those tiny little feet,
Your skin is soft, your eyes so blue,
I'm in awe when I look at you.

Baby, baby,
So small and cute,
Dressed in your bright little baby suit,
You're as happy as can be,
Your eyes always smiling and following me.

Baby, baby, baby, baby.

Lyndsay Scott (9)
Lilly Hall Junior School

SUN - KENNING

A star,
A powerhouse
A blistering baking bonfire,
An overpowered radiator
A spectacular sight

A globe of fire
A giant ever-burning candle.
A scorching, scolding sphere,
The heart of space
That gives us life.

Josh Tye (11)
Lilly Hall Junior School

DON'T

Don't slurp
Don't kiss
Don't burp
Don't miss
Don't scream
Don't shout
Don't run about
Don't cry
Don't kick
Don't lie
Don't get sick
Don't pull
Don't push.

Don't do anything you mustn't!

Lucy Williams (8)
Lilly Hall Junior School

THE CHRISTMAS ROBIN

His chest is a deep crimson red,
And his woolly jumper is brown,
He darts around the garden,
Observing every movement and sound,
He, the messenger of Christmas,
Just arrives and departs every winter,
When that cheery fellow disappears,
Springtime is upon us.

Michael Ward (11)
Lilly Hall Junior School

BRIGHT, SHINY, GLOWING GLITTERY NECKLACE

As good as a diamond
As bright as a sun
As shiny as a crystal
As glittery as a bee
As glowing as a light
As colourful as a rose
As pretty as a butterfly
As merry as a fly
As good as a you
As pretty as a me
As pleasant as a flower
I wish I could wear my necklace.

Laura Burton (8)
Lilly Hall Junior School

AUTUMN

Autumn's coming
Autumn's coming
Don't sit down, autumn's coming.
Trees are turning brown.
Chestnuts falling down.
Autumn's coming,
Autumn's coming,
Don't sit down,
Autumn's coming.

Blue Mullins (11)
Lilly Hall Junior School

BEDTIME

When I go upstairs to bed,
I usually give a loud cough.
This is to scare the monsters off.

When I come to my room,
I usually slam the door right back.
This is to squash the man in black
Who sometimes hides there.

Nor do I walk to the bed,
But usually runs and jumps instead.
This is to stop the hand -
Which is under there all night -
From grabbing my ankles.

Jessica Firth (9)
Lilly Hall Junior School

WAR POEM

The dreaded time
comes nearer and nearer.
The sadness comes to tears.
War is just about to start.
War, war,
what a terrible sight.
People lose their loved ones.
While the evil takes over.
War, war, war,
what a terrible sight you've ever seen.

Bronwyn Thomas (11)
Lilly Hall Junior School

IT IS HERE

At springtime you can smell the blossom falling off.
The sweet smell everywhere you go.
Spring is here
Spring you see.

Summertime burning hot
I'm going on holiday.
I've got a magnificent ice cream in my hand.
Red hot sun shining on me.
Summer you see.

Autumn time is here
Leaves falling off the trees.
Brown, yellow and red on the floor.
Autumn is here.
Autumn you see.

Winter is here.
Winter get your hat, your gloves and your scarf.
Fields of white.
Girls and boys having snowball fights.
Boots thudding into the snow.
Winter is here.
Winter you see.

Rachel McCabe (8)
Lilly Hall Junior School

THE WIND

The tree rustles in the wind like leaves blowing away.
The sound is cool and calming as flying and fluttering birds.
Nothing can beat the sound of the wind in the air.

Joe Kirk (9)
Lilly Hall Junior School

SNOW

When the snow falls
Our mothers always know,
Where we go by the footprints
In the snow.

Snow, is bitter cold,
Fell all the night.
And I woke to see
The garden white.

The snowflakes like diamonds,
Falling from the night sky.
Like white feathers fluttering
And still the silvery flakes go whirling by my face.

When the snow falls
Our mothers always know
Where we go by the footprints
In the snow.

Craig Allen (10)
Lilly Hall Junior School

THE SEA

The sea is blue,
The sea is green.
I wanted to see the sea,
But instead I had to have my tea.
I wanted to see the seashells
But instead there were some bells.
I wish I could see the sea,
It makes me feel so free.

Rachel Mangles (9)
Lilly Hall Junior School

HOT AND COLD

Venus has no moons, atmosphere of carbon dioxide gas,
Its heavy clouds trap the heat like greenhouse glass,
It's called the Evening Star because it shines like one with
a temperature of 480°C.
One day lasts 243 Earth days,. no time
Soon will Venus sleep.

Pluto, one moon, no atmosphere known
and furthest from the sun.
Temperatures at - 240°C when Earth's coldest recorded is - 89°C.
On Pluto would seem like a heatwave.
A landscape of rock covered with ice and a thin layer
of frozen methane,
One day on Pluto lasts just under one Earth week,
Soon Pluto will sleep.

Melissa Brown (11)
Lilly Hall Junior School

FOOTBALL CRAZY

Football crazy, football mad, is best and
Come and play with the lads.
Liverpool are before, then Leeds.
Michael Owen shoots and it's a goal.
Football crazy, football mad, football is best and
Come and play it with the lads.
Liverpool are going for the World Cup.
Liverpool are going for the World Cup.
Liverpool, Liverpool, Liverpool, Liverpool are the best.
            Football.

Callam Riley (8)
Lilly Hall Junior School

GLOWING SHELLS

In my grandma's garden there is a pretty little shell.
It's cream, round and swirly, it's a gorgeous little shell.
My grandma's got a shell, it is as white as snow.
It's small, thin and not very long.
She says she got it yesterday freshly from the sand.
She washed it and she cleaned it and it's a beautiful little shell.
Shining, glowing shell.

Tessa White (8)
Lilly Hall Junior School

THE THEME PARK

Once I went to a theme park.
The day was dull but windy.
I went to the spinning, whizzing Ferris wheel
It didn't cost a lot.
I begged to go on the Oblivion.
It made me feel like a bat upside down.
Then on to the rapids.

Ryan Hicks (8)
Lilly Hall Junior School

MOON

The moon is like a frosty ice cube.
The moon is like misty frost.
The moon is like a huge burger.
The moon wears a gigantic fluffy white coat.
The moon looks like a golf ball.
The moon lies in refreshing cold water.

Hayley Parker (10)
Lilly Hall Junior School

THE BRIGHT STARS

The stars are bright like a shining sun.
Shining in the sky.
Bright and glittery.
Shooting as fast as lightning.
Light as to l ight the dark and cloudy night sky.
As pointy as a pin
As hard as a stone!

Emma Wear (8)
Lilly Hall Junior School

MY RED ROBOT

Shiny red robot
Blue shoes
Bops up
Body moves
Speaks loudly
Eyes glow
It dances!

Eethan Parks (9)
Lilly Hall Junior School

THE SUN - KENNING

A morning welcomer
A light producer
A duster of repelling heat
A time maker
A forever burning star
A shining super star!

Samantha Rendi (10)
Lilly Hall Junior School

MY CAT ARTHUR

Arthur is black and white
At night he likes to fight,
He lays by the fire all day long,
Licking his paws with his rough tongue.

He has a girlfriend called Emmy.
But she is one of many,
Arthur thinks he's a real cool dude,
He makes sounds which are sometimes rude.

He's a cat who likes the sun
He likes to play and have his fun.
He sleeps in the day which is really a pain
But he is proud of his name.

Arthur's favourite food is rabbit
He eats it out of habit.
He often likes a piece of cheese,
For this he will always say, 'Please.'

He has a brother called Oscar
Who's a bit of an imposter.
He tries to steal Arthur's bed
Arthur instead pounces on his head.

Life without Arthur would be sad
In fact I would go mad.
Without his kindness
I would go mindless.

Megan Gomersall (10)
Lilly Hall Junior School

MY CAT

My cat is black and white.
Soft, cuddly and furry.
She is called Sophie.
She likes everybody to gently stroke her.
She is a softy.
She chases the frightened birds away.
She does not like the lashing rain on her.
Sophie is a very strange cat because she is not scared of dogs.
    Not at all!

Jacob Hamshaw (9)
Lilly Hall Junior School

I HAVE NO FRIENDS AT ALL

This morning I was new and had no friends at all.
I cried and cried and tried to hide.
I was alone.
But then you smiled 'Hello'
And invited me to play.
Now have you guessed the rest?
You're my best friend from today!

Emma Shaw & Toni Bellis (8)
Lilly Hall Junior School

WEATHER AND SEASONS

Spring is when the rain comes down
and when the daffodils spring up and shout -
'If you look you might see one or two bumblebees.'
Summer is when the sun comes up
and leaves spring from the trees.
Seas are blue, grass is green.

Autumn is when the leaves fall off the trees,
and when the leaves turn orange and brown.
Winter is when the snow falls down
and when the night dawns early.
Snow is falling through the night
and in the morning, snow will be on the ground.

Samantha Mullins (10)
Lilly Hall Junior School

TALKING TREE

When I was walking
I saw a tree talking.
Its trunk was brown like normal
Its leaves were green like all leaves are.
I've never seen a talking tree.
It blows in the wind like all trees do.
Its leaves come off in autumn too.
I've never seen a talking tree
Have you?

Abby Smith (10)
Lilly Hall Junior School

PLUTO - KENNING

A winter keeper
A freezing sunbather
A large freezer
An ice creator
A colossal iceberg
An ice guard!

Thomas Thompson (11)
Lilly Hall Junior School

SHELLS

Shells are twirly
Shells are still
They lay on the beach
All calm and still.
Put them in your ear
And you will hear
The sea just like real.
Once you hold one
You will never let go of it.
Shells can be used for
Making ornaments,
Decorating sandcastles,
Or putting in a shop
Shells are great!

Victoria Walker (9)
Lilly Hall Junior School

WINTER

Winter come in
Winter come in
Build a snowman
Winter come in
Freeze your sock off
Have a snowball fight
Winter come in
Winter come in
    Freeze!

Milly Mullins (8)
Lilly Hall Junior School

MY BEDROOM

Everything in place
Not one speck of dust
No pots on my desk
Nowhere a mouldy crust
My posters all up straight
Not a crease or curve in sight.

That's my dream! . . .

Jennie Bower (9)
Lilly Hall Junior School

MY FRIEND'S HOUSE

Squeaky floorboards
Creaky doors
My friend's scary toys looking at me
Knocking knees
Shivering with fright
Scary shadows I can see.

Noisy heaters
Cooling down
Scratching sounds under my bed
Cold draughts
Blowing in
Freezing cold around my head.

Tapping twigs
On the bedroom window
Branches banging gave me a fright
Wind howling
Lightning flashing
Will I ever fall asleep before the end of the night?

Luke Rhodes (9)
Rudston Preparatory School

A ROCKET TO MARS

The rocket stands upright on the launch site
smiling spacemen look to their flight
waiting to blast off into space
messengers of the human race.

Five, four, three, two, one
the engines begin their roaring song
flames and fire shower the ground
the rocket rises, red planet bound.

From here Earth is a million miles afar
twinkling in the darkness like a star
the sun is more distant too
and there's nothing much to do.

On to Mars now the size of the moon
we'll be landing soon
will we ever again see Earth
the land of our birth?

Sunlight streams through the window
and I stir on my bed below
thank goodness it's not what it seems
it's just one of my dreams.

Ben Daly (8)
Rudston Preparatory School

SILLY ME!

In the night, just laying there,
Shivering to the last piece of hair.
All alone in my bed,
Crazy thoughts going through my head.
In the corner I can see my chair
But where is my teddy bear?

Is that noise him moving around
Or just the clock making its sound?
What's that touching my leg?
'Don't get me!' I beg.
Jumping with fright, I feel unsteady
Silly me, it's just my old teddy.

Ben Booth (9)
Rudston Preparatory School

MY LITTLE SISTER IS INVISIBLE

I wake up in bed
No school today
It's Saturday
My little sister calls me
To her bedroom I go
She wants me to play
But where did she go?
I look around her bedroom
I look under the bed
She is nowhere to be seen
She is *invisible.*
I go downstairs
The piano is playing but no one is there
My sister calls me, I go in the room
The television is switched on
Somebody is watching cartoons
But where is my sister, she is not in this room?
I go in the kitchen
I go in the hall
She is nowhere to be seen
She is *invisible.*

Camilla Morte (8)
Rudston Preparatory School

CHICKENPOX

Chickenpox,
As red as a fox.
Those itchy, horrid, blotchy dots.
Those tiny, little, scratchy spots.

The dreaded calamine lotion,
A freezing icy potion.
The horrid taste of Medinol,
And yucky, nasty Calpol.

I'd much rather go to school,
Or have a swim in my local pool.
Girls' Games Club I really like,
And going to Brownies and riding my bike.

But *no,* chickenpox won't let me go!

I've missed the choir with Mr Gyte,
And we need to practise to get it right,
And if I don't go to drama today,
I won't be able to be in the play.

But *no,* chickenpox won't let me go!

Chickenpox is everywhere,
Some on my nose and some in my hair.
I try not to start to scratch,
It feels like a horrible, itching match.

I'm lying in my lonely bed,
With just the company of my ted.
But when it's gone I guess it's OK,
Then I'll be able to go out and play.

Emma R Taylor (9)
Rudston Preparatory School

THE BASEMENT OF NUMBER 64

The basement of number 64. No one knows what's there.
The things that are around you, they really make you stare.

I sneaked down to the basement to raid my stash of sweets
Not taking into consideration the things I just might meet.

But then I saw something in the corner with red glowing eyes.
I walked slowly towards it, afraid of a frightening surprise.

What was this strange manifestation?
I stretched out my arm numb with fear.
Not knowing what was lurking there.

The tips of my fingers touched it
It was soft, and suddenly it fell to the floor.
I turned on my torch and the light caught it.
It was teddy, my baby toy.

Alexander Allt (8)
Rudston Preparatory School

WHERE ARE MY FOOTBALL BOOTS?

Where are my football boots?
I have looked up and down all around.
I have looked under chairs and up on the stairs.
I have looked inside and outside all around.
I have looked everywhere they are nowhere to be found!
My dad keeps saying to make sure you check all around,
or in the match you won't score!
Losing my football boots is against the law!
Thank goodness my mum found them behind the door!

Hardeep Hothi (9)
Rudston Preparatory School

HIDDEN TREASURE

On a desert island Katie and I
With only a map in my hand
Find the point where we will start
To look for the hidden treasure.

One step right, ten steps left
Following the detail on the map
We shall follow all day long
Until it is too late to carry on.

Next morning we wake up
To carry on with the task
Step by step nearer we get
To find the big black cross.

Dig, dig, dig down and down
Until we hit the wooden box.
Open the lid, both of us
To find our great jackpot.

Thomas Pike (8)
Rudston Preparatory School

MY JENNY

Jenny is a monster
I tell you why
She nips people
But she's my Jenny
And I love her.

My Jenny is trouble
Lots of trouble
She's a pain
But she's my Jenny
And I love her.

My Jenny is caramel and sugar
She has sticky up ears
And a pointed tail
She's my Jenny
And I love her.

Amber Beardshall (8)
Rudston Preparatory School

HIDDEN TREASURE UNDER THE SEA

The day I went under the sea
My smile was big and full of glee.
Under the sea was my best friend and me
The day I went under the sea.

Looking for hidden treasure
Were me and my best friend Heather.
We did it all together
Looking for hidden treasure.

There were blue and red fish
Sitting in a dish
And after a very big swish
There were lots of purple fish.

At last we found the treasure
Me and my best friend Heather.
We did it all together
At last we found the treasure.

My trip under the sea
Tired out Heather and me
It left me full of glee
Did my trip under the sea.

Emma Taylor (9)
Rudston Preparatory School

BOYS

I hate boys.
Boys are weird,
I like girls better.

I hate boys.
They get on my nerves,
Boys think they're so smart!

Boys are disgusting
They like bugs,
but girls like being fancy in their frilly dresses.

Girls read or watch TV
Boys are too busy playing on their PlayStations.
Or, they play on their Game Boys for an hour!

There is always something stuck in my head.
Shall I tell you what it is?
I hate boys!

Charlotte Furniss (8)
Rudston Preparatory School

WHO WILL I BE?

When I grow up
Who will I be?
Doctor, dentist
Maybe
Scientist, soccer player
Yes please.
Who will I be?

Policeman, politician
We'll see.
Banker, baker
More buns please.
Astronaut, artist
Not any of these.
Perhaps I'll be, just me.

Christian Robinson (8)
Rudston Preparatory School

FOOTBALL INVADERS

Having a football match
Wednesday v Chelsea.
Chelsea winning 4-0.

Then high in the sky.
Bright lights shining down.

'What's that?' Wednesday shout.
All the Wednesday players were beamed up above.
Find themselves in an alien ship.

Intensive training for them all
Aliens aim to make them the best.

Return to Earth in a flash of light,
Continue the match.
Wednesday become the winners 5-4.

Wicked winning Wednesday!

Michael Akhavan Hezaveh (8)
Rudston Preparatory School

FOOTBALL BEATERS

The Football Beaters never lose,
Because of the skills they always use.
They take a shot and then they score,
The crowd all cheer at what they saw.
The game goes on and on and on,
Now the score is six to one.
Oh no a yellow card the referee shows,
One more time and one man goes.
The goalie saves every goal,
Except the one that got through the hole.
Now the end is very near,
Losing the game is not a fear.
Football Beaters win the game,
That is the reason they have that name.

Callum Faulkner (8)
Rudston Preparatory School

DRAGONS

Dragons can fly
Dragons do cry
They can fry chips in seconds
But eat beans and all kinds of greens
They look really strong
But can sing you a sweet song
I know, because my best friend is a one
You won't see him, because now he has gone
He is a space dragon!

Matthew Woods (8)
Rudston Preparatory School

I WAS IN SPACE

I had a dream it came true.
I was in space.
I jumped on the moon.
The stars were like glitter.
The moon was so bright.
Jupiter was so beautiful.
Mars was like a light.
I was in space, how could it be true?

Simon Parkin (9)
Rudston Preparatory School

SCARY MONSTER

Something there or maybe where?
Scary, scary - maybe hairy. A creak of a door,
A crack on the wall.
Flames appearing everywhere - striking flashes
Stop! Scary, worrying
Start crying - start running
Big or small or maybe tall
Cats asleep - didn't make a peep
Why not leap
Or maybe even creep?
Just pretend
And then you won't feel the heat.

Craig Johnson (10)
Trinity Croft CE Primary School

MOLES

What's that sound
Under the ground?

Is it a mole
Making a hole?

They all come out at night,
Where there is no light.

But if there is no light to be seen,
What could this mean?

It is very dark,
With no shining spark.

Kelly Freemantle (11)
Trinity Croft CE Primary School

WAR

War is *horrid*
War is *anger*
War is where my dad is!

War is *rage*
War is people in a cage.

War is *danger*
War is *evil*

War is where my dad is!

Leanne Longden (11)
Trinity Croft CE Primary School

THE MONSTER CAVE

A monster rave,
A bone shattering cave,
Hidden underground,
So you can't even hear a single sound,
A monster lives in it,
Just like a bear in a pit,
You'll run and run and run,
If you think it's a lot like fun.
You'll hear a moany sound,
I think the monster's name is -

    Sam.

Andrew Auty (10)
Trinity Croft CE Primary School

ANIMALS

Animals get a fright,
From dangers in the night,
Always on the run,
Bang! Bang! Bang!
Colours in the night,
That rush out of sight.

Fire in the light,
Roar! Roar! Roar!
In the night.

Stacie Lee (10)
Trinity Croft CE Primary School

GUESSING GAME

A furry ball,
A pink nose,
A friend indeed,
A small mouth full of small, sharp teeth,
Yes you've got it -

it's a hamster!

Lisa-Marie Greaves (11)
Trinity Croft CE Primary School

COOL SCHOOL

In the school of Victoria
At Christmas we sing Gloria.
The children are very bright,
The teachers are always right.
I have got a big pride, they always hide.
They like the special ride.
The little ones cried.

James McCarthy (8) & Sam Holmes (9)
Wath Victoria J&I School

IT'S ICY

It's icy, it's icy, so what shall I do?
I could put on my coat and my ice skates too.
I could skate on the pond and crack the thick ice
Then I'll get my friends and play very nice.
Then we'll play racing
And then chasing.
In the cold air, it is very bracing.

Chloe Mitchell & Daniel Hartshorn (8)
Wath Victoria J&I School

WHAT IS?

What is dog?
A dog is a fighter,
He makes me feel brighter.

What is cat?
A cat has whiskers
Tickles when she licks.

What is rabbit?
Hares are like rabbits,
Rabbits have bad habits.

Kelly Nunn & Catherine Spencer (8)
Wath Victoria J&I School

SCHOOL DAYS

Soon it will be school time
Catherine always likes to rhyme
Hat and gloves ready to go
On our way to call for Joe.
Often we climb trees
Lucky people get the breeze.
Dress in warm clothes so you don't freeze
And make sure you do your best.
Yes that's right!
Go to school!

Chloe Usher & Jodie Hayselden (8)
Wath Victoria J&I School

THE SHUT DOWN SCHOOL

In a misty old town there is a derelict school.
In the derelict school there are ghosts and ghouls.

No one dares go in the school.
They will get goosebumps - no fool would go in the school.

The councillor wanted it burnt down,
But they wouldn't; the councillor had a horrid frown,
And now all the school still standing - *shut down.*

Joshua Harrison & Joe-Elliott Hobson (9)
Wath Victoria J&I School

WHAT IS RED?

What is red? A rose is red
Where they stand in a bed.
What is yellow? Fruit's yellow
Where they are mellow.
What is pink? Lips are pink
When you go for a drink.
What is colourful? A rainbow is colourful
Where you stand and watch it.

Ashleigh Turner & Megan Soame (9)
Wath Victoria J&I School

WHAT IS BLUE?

What is blue? The sky is blue,
Where the clouds float thro'
What is white? A swan is white
Sailing in the light.

What is red? A poppy is red
In its barley bed.
What is violet? The clouds are violet
In summer twilight.

Charlotte Scales (8)
Wath Victoria J&I School

BORING!

I love school - *not!*
I hate it a lot.

School makes me bright
But everyone has a fight.

I only want to have some fun
It always rains, never any sun
Hurry up Miss! . . . I'm done.

Joanne Dawson (8)
Wath Victoria J&I School

COLOURS

If there were no colours what would I miss?

The bright green leaves waving in the wind.
The leaves floating gently to the ground and making a carpet.
The brown conkers dropping from the trees and them been picked.
The shining red applies glowing on the brown old trees.

I would miss the bright colours of the rainbow
When it has been sunny and raining.

Thomas Colton (8)
Wentworth CE Primary School

THE ANGRY RULING SEA

I crash and bash against the sea wall,
It makes me mad, because now I'm not tall.
I trip over children, who cry out their eyes,
But when I am happy, they splash on my thighs!

I shriek and shout, for there's no doubt
I am the lord of all the seashore.

In the past I've drowned many fishermen,
But nowadays I'm lucky to get ten!
Sometimes I cry, for my fish that are pie,
It makes me mad, as I need them back bad!

I shriek and shout, for there's no doubt,
I am the lord of all the seashore.

When it's sunny, I jump with joy!
But when it's grey, I really annoy!
When in the sun, I can be lots of fun,
But when there's rain, I will go insane!

I shriek and shout, for there's no doubt,
I am the lord of all the seashore.

My teeth are white foam, I don't need any bone!
A murky dark blue, my colour is too!

I shriek and shout, for there's no doubt,
I am the lord of all the seashore.

I'm not a bin, so don't perform such sin,
As littering me or you, will be *history!*

I shriek and shout, for there's no doubt,
I am the lord of all the seashore.

Samuel Beres (10)
Wentworth CE Primary School

THE GUARDING ABBEY

I am the guardian of the town,
I am the giant as I look down.

I stand on that hill like a guardian angel,
Watching over the town.
I look down feeling proud,
I glare at everyone admiring me.

I am the guardian of the town,
I am the giant as I look down.

I look at myself
I feel as though I am a paint pallet of colours.
I am terracotta, caramel and white,
Like a box of delicious chocolates.

I am the guardian of the town
I am the giant as I look down.

The weather has been tearing me,
It looks a like mouse has been nibbling my body,
It's been eating me.
All my flesh has gone now, I'm just a see-through skeleton.

I am the guardian of the town,
I am the giant as I look down.

I remember the days I was a guarding soldier
People honoured my beauty.
Then I got weaker,
My caramel stones disappeared
Until the birds started to swoop down on me.
Now I'm a ruin still standing,
As though I was the soldier that I used to be.

Victoria Fairclough (10)
Wentworth CE Primary School

WHITBY ABBEY

I guard the town below,
but I feel vulnerable as my crippled skeleton crumbles
in my face.
It upsets me at night so I cry and my tears crash to the ground.

I guard the town below.
I have altered it five hundred years so many people say.
From being a healthy abbey with no cold wound
that the wind echoes in,
to a model which is flashed at by cameras below.

I guard the town below.
I have a monopoly of chocolate colours covering me head to toe.
I say my bricks are like sweets because the wind every day
eats a sweetie.
I guard the town below.

Emily Peirson (11)
Wentworth CE Primary School

THE GUARDING ANGEL

I now feel hollow as time has washed me away.
I ached for ages when people took me apart
When I talk about the past I don't know where to start.

I look down on the town below,
I'm glad when people arrive and say hello.
I'm the guarding angel for Whitby
I stand up on the hill tall and proud.
When I got bombed I wanted to scream really loud.

The wind is my enemy when it wears my bricks away.
I used to have autumn colour leaves
I hope that it will stay.

Amber Travis (11)
Wentworth CE Primary School

DREAM

Sometimes I think
That there is a scary monster under my bed,
In the cupboard on a web.

Who else knows what
It feels like standing in the rain all on my own?

The spiders are slipping down my back.

I go through rain
When the rainbow is here
My eyes flash with colour.

Sometimes I wish that I was swimming on the water
With the dolphins.

Robyn Nicholson (9)
Wentworth CE Primary School

THE PARTY

Party poppers *bang!*
Girls singing with the records.
People pick at the cake.
Balloons pop making babies cry.
Babies throwing pieces of cake, *splatter!*
Children shout and scream.
Mums and dads laugh at the top of their voices.
Children playing musical chairs, *scrape, scrape!*
Presents falling down the stairs, *bish bosh!*
Clowns dancing on the floor, *bang!*
Children fight with water pistols.

Carl Webb (9)
Wentworth CE Primary School

WHO ELSE KNOWS?

Who else knows . . .
about how lonely I can be,
in my bedroom at night?

Who else knows . . .
about listening to spooky noises,
what can they be?
Hiding under my covers,
scared as can be.

Who else knows . . .
about the talking wardrobe
and the walking bookshelf,
in the gloomy night?

Who else knows . . .
about me in my bedroom at night?
I have a big fright . . .

Who else knows . . .
about the scratching branches,
outside in the dark?

Who else knows . . .
about the teddy bears dancing,
having a picnic in my room?

No one else knows . . .
about me lonely,
all alone,
in my bedroom at night.

Emily Cutts (7)
Wentworth CE Primary School

WHITBY ABBEY

As I gaze down as a guardian,
the town of Whitby is safe.
The unfixable eyes of gargoyles watch as the whirling sun swirls
through the clouds for me.

As I gaze down as a guardian,
My weak body will try to defeat anything in my path
as my sand falls from my stone.
I will protect fishermen from fierce seas as they catch their fish.

As I gaze down as a guardian,
My skeleton stands as a ruin,
The dangerous sea still eats away at me
while the wind and the rain helps rapidly
to devour my crumbling sandstone.

Alastair Jones (10)
Wentworth CE Primary School

SMELLY SEAWEED

When you are swimming in the sea,
You feel as if something is touching your belly
When you look down it's seaweed touching your belly.
It's very smelly,
It looks as though it's green jelly wrapping round your belly!

Jessica Higgins (7)
Wentworth CE Primary School

JUST ME

Sometimes I think there's someone there
Looking at me.

Who else knows that ghosts walk
round all night?

Who else knows that the trees
turn into aliens?

Who else knows about spiders
wriggling in my bed?

Who else knows about monsters
crawling up the drain?

Who else knows that my teddy bear
comes alive?

Who else knows toy soldiers march
up and down?

Who else knows about fairies dancing
on the rooftops?

Amelia Casagrande (8)
Wentworth CE Primary School

NOBODY KNOWS

Nobody knows how I felt, sitting in the grass, wet.
Nobody knows how sad I felt when I and the bully met.
Nobody knows how that boy always picked on me.
Nobody knows how often I hid behind a tree.
Nobody knows about the time when I scared *him* instead.
Nobody knows how frightened he is when *he* has to go to bed!

Rory Thompson (7)
Wentworth CE Primary School

GIANT OF THE WORLD

I am the giant of the world
I can be rough and nasty,
When fishermen empty my stomach
And take my fish from me.

I am the giant of the world,
I can be calm and gentle,
When children paddle on the beach
And make sandcastles just for me.

I am the giant of the world,
I strand people in my path,
They can never escape me,
Because they're gone quick and fast.

I am the giant of the world,
I have the greatest gift
Of keeping all the fish alive,
That's the important job of mine.

Charlotte Faith Cowen (11)
Wentworth CE Primary School

COLOURS

If there weren't any colours what would I miss?

The patterns on my horse's back and legs.
I like the pegs on my horse's saddle.
I also like the horses galloping in the woods.
I like the crusty colour of their legs and their manes.
Over the crusty golden floor the horses trot on their
white and brown legs.

Dyllon Walton (7)
Wentworth CE Primary School

THE RUINED ABBEY

Stand there tall and proud,
Which brings an awesome crowd!
The seagulls rest their nest on me but
I don't care, I'm doing a good deed.

I stand there tall and proud
Looking over sea, air and land.
People enter my body,
As an exciting hobby!

I stand there tall and proud
People used to worship in me
But now they say what '*history!*'

I stand there in bits and pieces,
I'm just a skeleton of the old me.
Still respected but not in the same way.

Leo Westmoreland (11)
Wentworth CE Primary School

I AM WHITBY'S GUARDIAN

I am Whitby's guardian,
Standing up so high.
I know that one day I will have to die,
Though I am getting old,
People say I look like gold,
I am told.

The wars against the wind and sea,
attack me with a sigh.
When I have been battered to bits,
I try hard not to cry.

Some do not respect me,
Some don't even care.
But when they come to see me again
I will get them, there!

Sam Bailey (10)
Wentworth CE Primary School

SEA

Who will be the next victim?
Crashing by the town I fly,
Always wet and never dry.

I split the countries from each other
And when I strike they take cover.
Whitby's shores are protected by the pier,
So I can't be rough in here.

Crashing by the town I fly,
Always wet and never dry.

In the past I've pulled people in,
But now they think I'm a litter bin.
I can be tougher than tin,
With my huge waves I'll drag them in.

Crashing by the town I fly,
Always wet and never dry.

But sometimes I'll let them play
And be rough another day.
The rain will splash on me,
Then I'll show how tough I can be.

Crashing by the town I fly,
Always wet and never dry.

Joshua Thompson (10)
Wentworth CE Primary School

WHITBY ABBEY

I am the giant of the Earth
I stand like a giant guarding the land
And see people moving up and down.
I look over the town and see children playing around.

I am the giant of the Earth
I sometimes feel quite lonely when the showery wet rain
Pours down on my brick tiered head,
But I know I won't be lonely again.

I am the giant of the Earth
I feel the rain eating away at me.
When I look back
There are holes in my vast walls.

I am the giant of the Earth
I've got one eye in the middle of my stone,
So I can watch and see I'm not alone.

Ruby Collins (9)
Wentworth CE Primary School

VALENTINE'S DAY

Valentine's Day is full of love.
Valentine's sight looks like a dove.
Valentine's love is everywhere.
Valentine's love is full of care.
Valentine's Day is very near so keep aware
because love is almost here!

Emily Thornhill (9)
Wentworth CE Primary School

WHO ELSE KNOWS . . .

Who else knows your furniture talks
when you sit on it?

Who else knows
how rulers turn into snakes?

Who else knows
clocks turn into ugly faces.

Who else knows
the pillow sucks your head
in when you're fast asleep?

Nobody knows about anything
because I am the only one in the world.

Luke Smith (8)
Wentworth CE Primary School

THE HEART OF WHITBY

I used to be a golden palace,
Now I'm cheese on toast.
I look down on the town
I used to be their favourite place to go.

During the fearsome winter,
The icy snow turned my body into a thick layer of crystals.
Now I'm a pile of multicoloured autumn leaves.

I stand towering above the town below
Proud and powerful like a king looking down on his kingdom.
I also get the aquatic sight off the ocean.
I protect the town from raging storms like a guardian of the town.

Adam Loveday (11)
Wentworth CE Primary School

DARKNESS

Darkness falls
Stars come out in the midnight sky.
Leaves scuttling down the street.
Someone's watching,
As I drift off to sleep.

Ronnie Postlethwaite (8)
Wickersley Northfield Junior School

DARKNESS

Darkness falls
Darkness falls in a black creepy room.
Black cat purring.
Cauldrons bubbling.
Snuggled up and warm in bed.

Alicia Karolewski (9)
Wickersley Northfield Junior School

DARKNESS

Nasty shadows make everyone jump.
Hedgehogs creeping through the woods.
Dark owls hooting for food.
Me shutting my eyes and having a good night's sleep.

William Cooper (8)
Wickersley Northfield Junior School

DARKNESS

Night begins,
A spooky moon hovers above me.
I lay awake in bed.
Wolves howl,

Clocks tick quietly,
Creepy shadows start appearing,
Lights disappear magically,
The whole world sleeps.

Laura Brown (8)
Wickersley Northfield Junior School

DARKNESS

Darkness falls
Like blinding sight.
Cats squealing, bats squawking
Floorboards creaking on the bathroom floor
Nervous as I hear the landing light flicker.

Dayle Maddison (9)
Wickersley Northfield Junior School

DARKNESS

Darkness falls and the shadows awaken.
The sun hides away and the moon comes out to play.
It feels like comforting black feathers wrapping around me
Making me warm as I go to sleep.

Amy Holmes (8)
Wickersley Northfield Junior School

DARKNESS

Darkness falls silently.
It feels like an underground mine.
I hear spooky footsteps on the stairs.
Feeling cold wrapped up in a blanket.

Michael Skelton (8)
Wickersley Northfield Junior School

WEATHERMAN

When I'm outside
It's as cold as Jack Frost doing his work
And as chilly as snow crackling beneath my feet.

When I'm inside,
I'm as warm as a chilli
Inside my mouth
And as hot as a blazing fire sparking in front of me.

Catherine Gleave (8)
Wickersley Northfield Junior School

DARKNESS

Darkness is falling
Daylight fades through the sky.
Someone shivers in gloomy, misty air.
Owls hoot and fly around.
I hear a creak on the stairs as I lay in bed.
I feel a breeze, the window is open.

Amy Taylor (8)
Wickersley Northfield Junior School

DARKNESS

Darkness falls like untouchable material.
Burglars creep in the hall.
Old men snore in their beds.
Creaks on your stairs.
Spiders scattering.
It makes me feel like scary stories.

Harriet Phillips (8)
Wickersley Northfield Junior School

DARKNESS

Darkness falls awakening devil shadows.
Wind making trees sway gently
Quietly tapping on the window
With their very slim fingers.

Lamp lights flickering
It feels like at night
A black sheet wraps around the world.

Dominic Cooling (9)
Wickersley Northfield Junior School

DARKNESS

Darkness falls like an endless tumble of pitch-black ribbons.
The shadow maker on the moon creates shadows on every house.
Shadows reappear on and off the walls.
Darkness turns on every street light to brighten up the night.
Floorboards creaking away, owls hooting,
Drifting away into the night.

Simon Witton (8)
Wickersley Northfield Junior School

DARKNESS

Darkness falls.
Scary shadows flicker on the walls.
Branches knock on the window.
Owls zooming past the window.
Feels like evil is coming.

Shannon Flannery (8)
Wickersley Northfield Junior School

DARKNESS

Darkness falls as the day dies down.
Dogs howl at the full moon.
Stars whizz and zoom across the sky.

Owls screeching and looking for food to give to its owlets.
An impatient lorry driver testing his horn.

It feels like an everlasting sleep that I will never wake up.
It feels like a soft sheet wrapping me up.

Abigail Ashworth (8)
Wickersley Northfield Junior School

DARKNESS

Darkness falls
Stars glow
Breezy as the wind
Tapping at your window
Turn off the lights
I feel scared.

Hannah Stewart (8)
Wickersley Northfield Junior School

DARKNESS

Darkness falls like flames
dying in the fire.
It sounds like a big black bat.
Flying in the night sky.
It feels like a cold, soft blanket,
covering the world.

Adam Nelson (8)
Wickersley Northfield Junior School

DARKNESS

Darkness falls,
bats hang on my tree.
The stars come out in the sky.
Creepy music thumps on my walls,
and a wolf howls in the street.
Darkness is like an eagle searching for prey
and like a life just ending.

Caroline Duncan (9)
Wickersley Northfield Junior School

DARKNESS

Darkness is like . . .
a pitch-black sheet
sliding down your back.

Clocks tick creepily
floorboards creak
the whistling wind blows.

Joshua Louch (8)
Wickersley Northfield Junior School

DARKNESS

Darkness is when spooky noises start.
The radiators thud.
Footsteps creep on the landing.

Darkness feels like a soft sheet
wrapping up the whole world.
A black cloud sending everybody to sleep.

Keeley Thompson Baker (9)
Wickersley Northfield Junior School

DARKNESS

Darkness is like a World War starting.
A car crash smashing
A new world just beginning.

Darkness makes my dog start howling,
Owls begin hooting,
Trees start whistling.
Darkness is as mysterious as an ancient ruin,
As gloomy as a cave,
As dark as a pitch-black sheet.

Daniel Law (8)
Wickersley Northfield Junior School

DARKNESS

Darkness falls
Owls flying, hunting rats and mice.
People talking, engines revving,
Warm and comfy,
Fast to sleep,
No noise at all.

Joel Willers (8)
Wickersley Northfield Junior School

DARKNESS

Darkness falls
Floorboards creak as shadows approach on the walls.
The wind blows making trees tap on the windows.
Scary sounds pass my door.
Terrified, I lie under my cover.

Katie Swales (9)
Wickersley Northfield Junior School

DARKNESS

Darkness is like a World that's starting,
A car crash is rushing
A new world   beginning.

Darkness makes my dog start barking,
Owls begin hooting,
Trees start whistling,
Darkness is   mysterious as an ancient
    as ghostly as   owl,
As dark as a pitch-black ocean.

Daniel Kaye (8)
Wickersley North Field Junior School

THUNDER

Thunder is
Crashing and rolling,
Rain falling,
Wind racing,
Flash storm,
Moon hiding.

Back there
late at night.

    Junior School

DARKNESS

Darkness is
Footsteps   as shadows approach
The wind blowing   making trees tap on the
Scary sounds   my door.
I am scared I have   under my cover.

Katie Shelley
Wickersley North Field Junior School